COFFEE CAKES

105 Wonderful Recipes

By Lauri Bonn

Illustrations by
Chris Bonn

MAREN PUBLISHING
Bend, Oregon

2000 Second Printing

Illustrations © 1998, 2000 by Chris Bonn.

Printed in the United States of America by Maverick Publications, Inc.

ISBN: 0-9665450-5-2

10 9 8 7 6 5 4 3 2

Illustrations by Chris Bonn

Cover Photograph by Gary Alvis

Front Cover: Fresh Blueberry Coffee Cake, page 76
Back Cover: Raspberry Cream Cheese Coffee Cake, page 122

Maren Publishing
PO Box 8205
Bend, OR 97708
(541) 383-2160
www.marenpublishing.com

CONTENTS

Introduction

One of my favorite ways to welcome Sunday morning is to be lured downstairs by a delicious aroma wafting room to room, enticing me to the kitchen to retrieve a freshly baked coffee cake from the oven. After cutting a piece of steaming hot cake, I pour myself a cup of coffee, and relax into a cozy chair with my favorite reading material or music. Sunday breakfast prepared!

Coffee cakes are great served alone or with eggs, hashbrowns, fruit, yogurt, or whatever constitutes a good breakfast to you. Some coffee cakes are basic and simple, while others are beautiful, elegant presentations. Coffee cakes may be made in advance and frozen. Most are easy enough to make just before breakfast is served.

Included are a wide variety of coffee cakes, plus a few of my favorite breakfast breads. If you are attracted to a certain recipe, but don't like a particular ingredient, leave out whatever it is that doesn't appeal to you. Whatever your likes, you are sure to find a few favorites within these pages.

The beauty of coffee cakes is that you do not have to be a master baker in order to prepare one (I am not). Most of them are simple, mix-it-up, put-it-in-a-pan, bake-it, and eat-it cakes. The toppings are generally your basic sprinkle-over- the-top-before-you- bake-it types.

Included are easy to read, step-by-step instructions with the ingredients and directions in sequential order for your baking ease.

Acknowledgments

One Sunday morning I woke up contemplating which coffee cake to make and the fact that I had no one source for coffee cake recipes. My husband, Mike, barely awake, suggested that I write a coffee cake cookbook. I would like to thank him for that inspiration and for standing behind me and supporting me on my journeys. My sons Carey and Tony have been most patient with my long hours at the computer. I thank my son, Chris, for his beautiful illustrations he managed to put together between classes at the University of Oregon.

Gary Asher of Maverick Publications was wonderful for giving me such useful information in which to begin my journey and bountiful assistance through to completion, including printing the second printing. Carla Wigle generously provided technical guidance and equipment of which I am incredibly grateful. My friend, Janet Johnson, with her impeccable taste and infectious excitement for my book was invaluable. Karen Meece for her ongoing spiritual nurturing, Lisa Faseler, and members of the BBA test kitchen, thank you!

Many thanks to my sisters Louise Johnson and Eileen Spencer for their recipes and encouragement; my brother Edward Bonn and his wife Cynthia for their generous support; my late parents Paul and Grace Bonn for their unconditional love and unwavering confidence in me; my sister Mary, a <u>true</u> master baker/artist who is always with me.

And, finally, to those of you who by various means assisted or even just gave me words of encouragement, thank you so much for your positive energy.

Tips

Coffee cakes are easy to make, requiring no special talent or knowledge to create a tasty masterpiece fit for a crowd of any sort. And it doesn't have to be a tedious or messy job. I will suggest couple of ways that may make it easier and help you keep your kitchen a little cleaner as you bake.

A wonderful aspect of coffee cakes is that the majority of them are baked and served out of the same pan. You don't layer them, frost them, or decorate them. The work is done by the time you put the cake in the oven to bake. Coffee cakes are often easier to make than cookies.

I'm pretty unfanatical about the way I bake. As long as the essential ingredients are included, such as baking powder, sugar, flour, etc., it's pretty hard to ruin a coffee cake. I think the ingredients used are much more important than the way the cake is put together.

For instance, all my recipes call for **butter**, because that's all I buy - I think it tastes better and, I believe, is healthier than margarine. But, feel free to use margarine, if that's what you prefer or have on hand. So I say, relax, have fun, and enjoy your creation.

The **flour** I use is unbleached, all-purpose.

Sifting flour - rarely do I sift. Depends on the day, if I'm in a hurry, and how much of a mess I want to make (mess is the key word here). Sifting the flour can make the consistency of the cake finer, which is why most desert cakes call for sifted flour. However, most coffee cakes are eaten hot and never get a chance to become dense. An alternative to sifting is to lightly spoon the flour into a measuring cup. Be careful not to pack it by shaking or tapping the measuring cup, then level off the top with a straight edge knife. The cake will probably not be noticeably different. I've never had anyone decline my baking because I didn't sift! However, many of these recipes instruct us to sift, so let me say that if you are a person who thinks it necessary to sift - great! Sift and be happy!

Baking time varies. Set your timer for a little less time than what the recipe calls for, and then check the cake. If your oven runs a little hot, you may want to turn it down a little.

The thing about **nuts**. I like nuts. My family does not. So I simply leave them out all together or put them on part of whatever I'm baking. Nuts are always optional.

Vanilla - only the real stuff. To me, it's like butter. Real is usually better than artificial. The fewer items in the ingredients list, the better.

The **eggs** in all these recipes are large.

Corn flakes make a great topping, so I keep a box of Corn Flake Crumbs in my cupboard. Corn flake cereal is great if you happen to have it on hand.

Greased pan - The easiest way to grease a pan it to take a stick of butter, still wrapped in paper, undo one end and slide it over the bottom of the pan until completely covered with a thin layer.

Maintaining a neat kitchen when you bake is made easier by having a sink full of clean, soapy water and putting ingredients, such as flour, salt, sugar, etc. away as you use them. By the time you are finished with your cake, all you have to do is wipe off the counters and wash the dishes.

Utensils

Following are certain basic utensils sure to make your baking life easier. Some are necessary for your sanity and others are just nice to have. These items are referred to in many of the recipes.

Measuring spoons and **measuring cups**, of varying sizes.

Wooden spoon - medium sized, that you only use for batters. You wouldn't want to share this spoon with a curry.

Pastry blender - a tool with rigid, curved wires, used to cut butter into flour.

Round layer cake pans - 8-inch or 9-inch.

Square cake pan - 8x8-inch or 9x9-inch, preferably glass.

Oblong cake pan - 9 1/2x13, preferably glass.

Pie plates - 9-inch, preferably glass.

Loaf pan - 9x5x3-inch, for baking bread.

Tube pan - 10x4-inch. Also used for Angel Food Cakes.

Bundt pan - 10-inch. A style of tube pan with fluted edges.

Springform pan - 8-inch or 9-inch round pan with removable sides.

Wire rack - comes in different sizes, for cooling cakes and cookies.

❦ALASKAN BLUEBERRY COFFEE CAKE❧

Cake:
1 1/2 cups flour
   3/4 cup sugar
2 1/2 tsp. baking powder
   3/4 tsp. salt
   1/4 cup butter, melted
   3/4 cup milk
      1 egg
1 1/2 cups fresh Alaskan blueberries (may use any fresh
      blueberries)

Topping:
   1/3 cup flour
   1/2 cup brown sugar, firmly packed
   1/2 tsp. cinnamon
   1/4 cup butter

Preheat oven to 375 degrees.

For cake, in a medium bowl, mix together flour, sugar, baking powder, salt; add butter, milk, egg, and 1 cup blueberries. Beat until thoroughly mixed (about 30 seconds) and pour into a greased 8x8-inch pan.

For topping, combine flour, brown sugar, cinnamon, and butter. Sprinkle over batter and top with the remaining 1/2 cup berries. Bake for 25 to 30 minutes, until just done. Best served warm.

Just when you're beginning to think it's going to burn, because the center isn't done, it firms up. The brown sugar makes a delicious crust and the blueberries don't have to come from Alaska! I love this one.

❧ALMOND STREUSEL COFFEE CAKE❧

Cake:
   1/2 cup butter, softened
   1/2 cup sugar
      3 eggs
      1 tsp. grated orange peel
   1/2 tsp. vanilla
      2 cups flour
      1 tsp. baking powder
      1 tsp. baking soda
   2/3 cup orange juice

Streusel:
   1 cup light-brown sugar, firmly packed
   1 cup sliced almonds
1/4 cup flour
   3 T. butter, melted
   1 tsp. grated orange peel

Glaze:
   1/2 cup confectioners sugar
2 1/2 tsp. orange juice

Preheat oven to 350.

For cake, in a large bowl, beat together butter and sugar until light and fluffy. Add eggs, one at a time, beating well after each addition using an electric mixer on medium speed. Beat in orange peel and vanilla. In a medium bowl, mix together the flour, baking powder, and baking soda.

On low speed, alternately beat flour mixture and orange juice into butter mixture, beginning and ending with flour. Spoon half of the batter into greased 9- or 10-inch tube pan.

For streusel, in a medium bowl, mix together brown sugar, nuts, and flour. Stir in the butter and orange peel. Sprinkle half the streusel over half the batter. Top with the remaining batter and streusel. Bake 30 to 35 minutes, or until a toothpick inserted in center comes out clean. Place pan on a wire rack to cool completely. Remove cake from pan onto a serving plate, placing it right-side up.

To prepare the glaze, in a small bowl or cup, stir together confectioners sugar and orange juice until smooth. Drizzle over the top of the warm cake.

❧APPLE ALMOND COFFEE CAKE❧

Cake:
    2 cups flour
2 1/4 tsp. baking powder
    1/4 tsp. salt
    1/2 cup butter, softened
      1 cup sugar
    1/2 cup milk
      2 eggs
1 1/2 tsp. vanilla extract
    1/2 tsp. almond extract

Topping:
    2 medium apples, Granny Smith, Golden Delicious, or
      Braeburn
    1/3 cup apple jelly
     1 T. sliced almonds

Preheat oven to 450 degrees.

In small bowl, mix flour, baking powder, and salt. In large bowl, beat the butter, adding sugar, milk, eggs, vanilla, and almond extract. Add flour mixture and beat on medium speed for 2 minutes or until smooth. Spread batter in a greased and floured 8-inch springform pan.

Peel, quarter, and core the apples. Cut each apple quarter into 1/2 inch-thick wedges. Arrange the apple wedges overlapping slightly in a circular pattern over the batter. Brush the apples with **half** the apple jelly. Sprinkle the almonds around the edge and in the center of the cake.

Bake for 15 minutes. Reduce the oven temperature to 350 degrees. Bake for 50 to 60 minutes longer, or until a toothpick inserted near the center comes out clean. (The cake will rise higher in the center).

Set the pan on a wire rack to cool for 15 minutes, then remove the side of the pan. Brush the top of the cake with the remaining apple jelly. Cool completely on the rack. Serve at room temperature.

❧APPLE COFFEE CAKE❧
with Hot Buttered Rum Sauce

Cake:

GREAT!

- 1/2 cup butter, softened
- 2 cups sugar
- 2 eggs
- 2 cups flour
- 1 tsp. baking powder
- 3/4 tsp. baking soda
- 1/2 tsp. salt
- 1/2 tsp. nutmeg
- 1/2 tsp. cinnamon
- 1 1/2 cups chopped walnuts (opt.)
- 3 cups peeled diced apples (3 to 4 apples)

Sauce:

- 1 cup sugar
- 1/2 cup light cream or half and half
- 2 T. butter
- 1/4 cup dark rum (or to taste)

Preheat oven to 350 degrees.

In a mixing bowl, beat butter and sugar until creamy. Add the eggs one at a time. Combine the flour, baking powder, baking soda, salt, nutmeg, and cinnamon; add gradually to the creamed mixture. Add the nuts and apples. Bake in a well-greased and floured tube pan for 60 minutes or until tests done. After 15 minutes invert onto a rack to cool.

Heat the sugar and cream over low heat until well-dissolved. Add the butter and rum. Serve hot over the cake.

Wonderfully moist ... the rum sauce makes this an outrageous holiday cake!

ꙹAPPLE COFFEE CAKEꙶ

Cake:
- 3 cups flour
- 1 T. baking powder
- 1 tsp. salt
- 1 cup sugar
- 1/2 cup butter, softened
- 3 eggs
- 1 1/2 cups milk
- 20 oz. can apple pie filling
- 2 tsp. cinnamon

Topping:
- 1/4 cup brown sugar, firmly packed
- 1/4 cup chopped nuts (opt.)
- 2 T. butter, melted

Preheat oven to 350 degrees.

In a medium bowl, combine the flour, baking powder, and salt. In a large mixing bowl, add sugar to butter; add eggs and milk; add dry ingredients to this mixture and beat on low speed of the mixer for 30 seconds. Beat at medium speed for 2 minutes. Pour half of the batter into a greased 9x13-inch pan. Combine the pie filling and cinnamon. Spoon half of the pie filling over the batter. Repeat with the remaining batter and pie filling.

For topping, combine the brown sugar and nuts, and sprinkle over the pie filling mix. Drizzle with melted butter. Bake until a wooden toothpick inserted in the center comes out clean. Serve warm.

❧APPLE NUT COFFEE CAKE❧

Cake:
1/2 cup butter, softened
  1 cup sugar
  2 eggs
  1 tsp. vanilla
  2 cups flour
  1 tsp. baking powder
  1 tsp. baking soda
1/2 tsp. salt
  1 cup sour cream
  2 cups finely chopped apples

Topping:
1/2 cup chopped nuts (opt.)
1/2 cup brown sugar, firmly packed
  1 tsp. cinnamon
  2 T. flour

Preheat oven to 350 degrees.

For cake, in a mixing bowl, cream together the butter and sugar. Add the eggs and vanilla and beat well. Sift (or don't sift!) together flour, baking powder, baking soda, and salt; add to butter mixture alternately with the sour cream. Fold in the chopped apple and spread the batter into a greased 9x13-inch pan.

For topping, in a small bowl, combine the nuts, brown sugar, cinnamon, and flour; mix well. Sprinkle over the batter. Bake for 35 to 40 minutes, or until tests done.

For my guys that don't like "stuff" in their coffee cakes, i.e. nuts, apples, etc., I leave out the nuts and chop the apples fine. They don't even realize there are apples in the cake, but the apples are what makes the cake very moist. It's quickly eaten.

◈APPLE ORANGE COFFEE CAKE◈

Filling:
    6 apples (3 cups peeled, cored, and sliced)
    5 T. sugar
    5 tsp. cinnamon

Cake:
    3 cups flour
    2 cups sugar
    1 T. baking powder
3/4 tsp. salt
    1 cup oil
    4 eggs
1/4 cup orange juice
    1 T. vanilla

Whipped cream

Preheat oven to 375 degrees.

Combine the apples sugar and cinnamon; set aside.

Sift the flour, sugar, baking powder, and salt into a bowl. Make a well in the center and pour in the oil, eggs, orange juice, and vanilla. Beat with a wooden spoon until well blended.

Spoon one-third of the batter into a greased angel food pan. Make a ring of half the drained apple mixture on top of batter, making sure not to have any apple touching sides of pan or they will stick. Spoon another third of the batter over, make a ring of the remaining apples and top with remaining batter. Bake 75 minutes or until done. Cover top with foil if top begins to over-brown.

Allow to cool slightly in pan before removing to a serving plate. Serve immediately with whipped cream.

❧APPLE PEAR COFFEE CAKE❧

Cake:
   1/2 cup butter, softened
     1 cup sugar
     2 eggs
     1 tsp. vanilla
     2 cups flour
     1 tsp. baking powder
     1 tsp. baking soda
  3/4 tsp. salt
     8 oz. sour cream
1 1/4 cups peeled, finely chopped cooking apples
       (about 2 apples)
  3/4 cup peeled, finely chopped pear
       (about 1 pear)

Topping:
     1 cup brown sugar, firmly packed
   1/2 cup chopped pecans (opt.)
     2 T. butter, softened
     1 tsp. cinnamon

Preheat oven to 350 degrees.

For cake, on medium speed of an electric mixer, cream butter and sugar; add eggs, one at a time, beating well after each addition; add vanilla. Combine flour, baking powder, baking soda, and salt; add to creamed mixture alternately with sour cream, beginning and ending with flour mixture. Fold in apple and pear. Spread batter in a greased 9x13-inch baking pan.

For topping, combine brown sugar, pecans, butter, and cinnamon; sprinkle evenly over batter. Bake for 45 to 50 minutes or until a toothpick inserted in center comes out clean.

ꕥAPPLESAUCE COFFEE CAKEꕔ

Cake:
   1/2 cup butter or oil
   1/4 cup sugar, brown or white
     1 egg
     1 cup applesauce, sweetened
   1/2 cup buttermilk
     1 cup white flour
     1 cup whole wheat flour
1 1/2 tsp. baking soda
     1 tsp. salt
     1 tsp. cloves
     1 tsp. cinnamon

Topping:
nutmeg, raisins, nuts - all optional

Preheat oven to 375 degrees.

Cream together butter, sugar, egg, applesauce, and buttermilk. Mix together flours, baking soda, salt, cloves, and cinnamon; add to butter mixture. Do not over mix, as in muffins.

Pour into greased 9x13-inch pan.

May sprinkle with topping. Bake for 30 minutes.

I found this recipe in my mom's recipe box - it's an oldie. Thanks mom!!

❧APRICOT STREUSEL COFFEE CAKE❧

Filling:
    1 cup finely chopped, dried apricots
    6 oz. package (1 cup) butterscotch chips
  1/2 cup water

Cake:
1 1/2 cups flour
    2 tsp. baking powder
  1/2 tsp. salt
  1/4 cup butter, softened
  1/2 cup sugar
    1 egg, slightly beaten
  1/2 cup milk

Streusel Topping:
  1/4 cup dark-brown sugar, firmly packed
    1 T. flour
  1/2 tsp. cinnamon
  1/2 cup finely chopped pecans (opt.)
    1 T. melted butter

Preheat oven to 375 degrees.

For filling, combine apricots, butterscotch chips, and water. Cook over moderate heat, stirring occasionally, until thick, about 10 minutes. Cool.

For cake, sift together flour, baking powder, and salt. Into butter, gradually add sugar and beat until fluffy. Add egg and beat thoroughly. Stir in milk and mix well. Add dry ingredients and mix well. Pour about two-thirds of the batter into a greased and floured 9-inch square pan.

Spread cooled apricot filling over top of batter. Drop remaining batter in small spoonfuls over filling.

For streusel topping, combine brown sugar, flour, cinnamon, pecans, and melted butter. Sprinkle over the top of the batter. Bake 20 to 25 minutes. Cool slightly before cutting.

❦APRICOT ALMOND COFFEE CAKE❧

Cake:
    1 cup butter, softened
    2 cups sugar
    2 eggs
    1 tsp. almond extract
    2 cups flour
    1 tsp. baking powder
  1/2 tsp. salt
    8 oz. sour cream

Filling/Topping:
    1 cup sliced almonds
    1 10-oz. jar apricot preserves (may try other types)

Preheat oven to 350 degrees.

For cake, beat butter until creamy. Gradually add sugar, beating on medium speed 5 to 7 minutes. Add eggs, one at a time, beating mixture just until yellow disappears. Add almond extract.

Combine flour, baking powder, and salt; add to butter mixture alternately with sour cream mixing on low speed, beginning and ending with flour mixture. Place one-third of batter into a greased and floured 12-cup Bundt pan.

Sprinkle with half of almonds, and dot with half of apricot preserves. Top with remaining batter; sprinkle with remaining almonds, and dot with remaining preserves.

Bake for 50 to 55 minutes, or until a toothpick inserted in center comes out clean. Cool in pan on a wire rack 10 to 15 minutes; remove from pan, and let cool completely on wire rack.

❦BANANA BREAD❧

 1/3 cup butter, softened
  1 cup sugar
  2 eggs
1 1/2 cup mashed ripe bananas (3 to 4 medium)
  1/3 cup water
1 2/3 cups flour
  1 tsp. baking soda
  1/4 tsp. baking powder
  1/4 tsp. salt
  1/2 cup chopped nuts (opt.)

Preheat oven to 350 degrees.

Using shortening, thoroughly grease the bottom of a 5x9-inch loaf pan; set aside.

In large bowl, mix butter and sugar; stir in eggs. Mix until blended. Add mashed bananas and water. Beat for 30 seconds. Stir in flour, baking soda, baking powder, and salt. Mix well. Stir in nuts. Pour into pan. Bake for about 55 to 60 minutes, or until a toothpick inserted in the center comes out clean.

When bread is done, place pan on a wire rack and let cool for about 5 minutes. Remove bread from pan; transfer bread to wire rack and let stand until it is completely cool.

This bread is very good toasted and buttered. Yum!

﹌BLUEBERRY BUCKLE﹌

Cake:
    1/2 cup butter, softened
    3/4 cup sugar
     1 egg
    2 cups flour
2 1/2 tsp. baking powder
    1/4 tsp. salt
    1/2 cup milk

Topping:
     2 cups blueberries
    1/2 cup sugar
    1/2 cup flour
    1/2 tsp. cinnamon
    1/4 cup butter

Preheat oven at 350 degrees.

For cake, cream together butter and sugar; add egg. Beat until light and fluffy. Sift together flour, baking powder, and salt. Add to creamed mixture alternately with milk. Spread in greased 9x9-inch pan.

Spread berries over batter. Mix sugar, flour, and cinnamon. Cut in butter until crumbly. Sprinkle over berries. Bake 45 minutes, or until done.

Always a favorite...

❧BLUEBERRY COFFEE CAKE❧

Cake:
2/3 cup butter
   1 cup sugar
   3 eggs, separated
   3 cups sifted flour
   2 tsp. baking powder
1/2 tsp. salt
   1 cup milk
   1 package (10 oz.) sweetened, frozen
       blueberries, thawed and drained

Topping:
1/4 cup brown sugar

Preheat oven to 350 degrees.

For cake, cream together butter and sugar; add egg yolks; beat until creamy. Sift flour again with the baking powder and salt. Add dry ingredients alternately with milk to butter mixture, mixing until well blended after each addition. Stir in drained blueberries. Beat egg whites until they form stiff peaks; fold into batter and pour into a greased 9-inch square pan.

Sprinkle brown sugar evenly over top, and bake for 34 to 40 minutes. Serve warm.

❧BLUEBERRY CRUMB CAKE❧

Cake:
    3 cups firm ripe blueberries
2 1/2 cups flour
    1 T. baking powder
    1/2 tsp. nutmeg
    1/4 tsp. cloves
    3/4 tsp. salt
    1/2 cup butter, softened
    1 cup sugar
    3 eggs
    3/4 cup milk

Topping:
    1/2 cup butter, chilled
    3/4 cup flour
    1 cup sugar
    1 tsp. cinnamon

    2 cups heavy cream

Preheat oven to 375 degrees.

Wash blueberries under cold water. Spread on paper towels and pat completely dry with clean towels.

For cake, into a bowl, sift together the flour, baking powder, nutmeg, cloves, and salt. In a separate bowl, cream together butter and sugar until they are light and fluffy. Beat in the eggs, one at a time. Add flour mixture alternately with milk, a third at a time, beating well after each addition. Gently fold in the blueberries. Pour the blueberry batter into a greased and floured 9x13-inch pan.

For crumb topping, cut the butter into 1/4 inch bits. Combine with flour, sugar, and cinnamon. Use a pastry blender until mixture is course and crumbly. Spread evenly over cake. Bake for 40 to 50 minutes or until cake tests done.

Serve warm with cream served in a separate pitcher.

❧BLUEBERRY CRUMBCAKE with Lemon❧

Filling:
  12 oz. frozen blueberries, thawed, undrained
   1 T. cornstarch
   1 tsp. grated lemon peel

Cake:
   2 cups prepared biscuit mix
   2 T. sugar
   2 T. butter
   1 egg
1/4 cup milk

Topping:
1/2 cup prepared biscuit mix
1/4 cup sugar
   1 tsp. cinnamon
   2 T. butter, softened

Preheat oven to 400 degrees.

In small saucepan, combine blueberries, cornstarch, and lemon peel. Cook, stirring, over medium heat, until mixture begins to boil and becomes thick and translucent. Let cool. May put in refrigerator while batter is being prepared.

For cake, in medium bowl, combine biscuit mix and sugar. With pastry blender or 2 knives, cut in butter until mixture resembles course crumbs. Add egg and milk, stirring until thoroughly combined. Pat dough on bottom and three quarters of the way up side of greased 9-inch round layer cake pan. Pour blueberry mixture over the dough.

For topping, in small bowl, combine biscuit mix, sugar, cinnamon, and butter. Mix with fork, until mixture is crumbly. Sprinkle evenly over blueberry mixture. Bake 20 minutes, or until topping is golden. Cool on wire rack. To serve, cut into wedges. Best served warm.

A luscious cake...hard to stay away from.

✺BLUEBERRY PECAN COFFEE CAKE✺

Cake:
    1 cup butter
    1 cup sugar
    2 eggs
    8 oz. sour cream
    1 tsp. vanilla
    2 cups flour
    1 tsp. baking powder
    1 tsp. baking soda
    1 21-oz. can blueberry pie filling

Topping:
    1/4 cup flour
    1/4 cup sugar
    3 T. butter
    1/2 cup pecans (opt.)

Preheat oven to 375 degrees.

For cake, cream butter; gradually add sugar. Beat until light and fluffy. Add eggs one at a time; beat well after each addition. Stir in the sour cream and vanilla. Combine flour, baking powder, and baking soda; gradually add to the creamed mixture, beating well after each addition. Spread half the batter in a greased 9x13-inch pan. Over this spread the pie filling, then the remaining batter.

For the topping combine the flour and sugar. Cut in the butter until the mixture resembles course crumbs. Stir in the pecans and sprinkle over the cake batter. Bake for 45 minutes.

Delicious, bakery quality cake - wonderful with the nutty flavor of pecans.

❧BLUEBERRY SOUR CREAM COFFEE CAKE❧

Cake:
1/2 cup butter, softened
    1 cup sugar
    3 eggs
    1 tsp. vanilla
    2 cups flour
    1 tsp. baking powder
    1 tsp. baking soda
1/2 tsp. salt
    1 tsp. ground cardamom (opt.)
    1 cup sour cream
    2 cups blueberries

Filling:
1/2 cup brown sugar

Preheat oven to 325 degrees.

For cake, cream butter and sugar; add eggs one at a time, beating well after each addition; add vanilla. Sift flour, baking powder, baking soda, salt, and cardamom together. Add flour mixture gradually to the egg mixture, alternating with sour cream and ending with the flour mixture. Fold 1 cup blueberries into the batter. Pour half the batter into a well greased and floured 9x13-inch pan.

Spread remaining blueberries over batter. Sprinkle with brown sugar and top with remaining batter.

Bake for 50 to 60 minutes, or until toothpick comes out clean.

BLUEBERRY POPPY SEED BRUNCH CAKE

Cake:
    2/3 cup sugar
    1/2 cup butter, softened
    2 tsp. grated lemon peel
    1 egg
1 1/2 cup flour
    2 T. poppy seeds
    1/2 tsp. baking soda
    1/8 tsp. salt
    1/2 cup sour cream

Filling:
    2 cups fresh or frozen blueberries,
        thawed, drained on paper towels
    1/3 cup sugar
    2 tsp. flour
    1/4 tsp. nutmeg

Glaze:
    1/3 cup powdered sugar
1 to 2 tsp. milk

Preheat oven to 350 degrees.

In large bowl, beat sugar and butter until light and fluffy. Add lemon peel and egg; beat 2 minutes at medium speed. In medium bowl, combine flour, poppy seeds, baking soda, and salt; add to butter mixture alternately with sour cream. Spread batter over bottom and 1 inch up sides of greased and floured 9- or 10-inch springform pan, **making sure batter on sides is 1/4 inch thick.**

For filling, in medium bowl, combine blueberries, sugar, flour, and nutmeg; spoon over batter. Bake at 350 for 35 to 45 minutes or until crust is golden brown. Cool 10 minutes. Remove sides of pan.

In small bowl or cup, combine powdered sugar and enough milk to make glaze desired drizzling consistency; stir until smooth. Drizzle over top of warm cake. Serve warm or at room temperature.

Very attractive display, a hint of lemon...

✺BUTTERMILK COFFEE CAKE✺

Cake:
2 1/4 cups sifted flour
  1/4 tsp. salt
  1/2 tsp. cinnamon
    1 cup brown sugar, firmly packed
  3/4 cup sugar
  3/4 cup oil
    1 tsp. soda
    1 tsp. baking powder
    1 egg, slightly beaten
    1 cup buttermilk

Topping:
    3/4 cup of first 6 ingredients
    1/2 cup walnuts, coarsely chopped (opt.)
      1 tsp. cinnamon

Preheat oven to 350 degrees, or 325 degrees for glass pan.

Combine flour, salt, and cinnamon into large bowl of electric mixer. Add brown sugar, sugar, and oil. Mix on medium speed until light and fluffy. **Set aside 3/4 cup of this mixture for the topping.** To the remaining mixture, add soda, baking powder, egg, and buttermilk; mix until smooth. Spoon mixture evenly into a greased 9x13-inch pan.

For topping, combine reserved mixture, nuts, and the 1 teaspoon of cinnamon. Sprinkle evenly over the top and press lightly with the back of a spoon. Bake for 25 to 30 minutes or until tests done. Serve warm.

A dense, not-too-sweet, nice flavored cake - easy to make!

⚬BUTTERMILK COFFEE CAKE⚬

(Bishop's Bread)

Cake:
>   2 cups flour
> 1 1/2 tsp. baking powder
>   1 cup light-brown sugar
>   3/4 cup butter, cut into small pieces
>   2/3 cup buttermilk
>   1 egg, lightly beaten
>   1/2 cup finely chopped pecans or almonds
>   1 tsp. cinnamon
>   1/2 cup currants

Topping:
>   1/2 cup of first 4 ingredients

Preheat oven to 425 degrees.

In a large mixing bowl, combine the flour, baking powder, brown sugar; cut in butter pieces using a pastry blender or two knives until they are the consistency of fine crumbs. **Take out 1/2 cup of this mixture to be used for the topping; set aside.**

Into the cake mixture, gradually stir in the buttermilk, egg, nuts, cinnamon, and currants. Mix thoroughly until the batter is smooth; pour into a greased and floured 9-inch round pan.

For topping, sprinkle the reserved crumb mixture evenly over the top of the batter. Bake for 15 minutes, then reduce the heat to 375 degrees. Bake for an additional 20 to 25 minutes, or until a toothpick inserted in the center comes out clean. Serve warm or room temperature.

❧CARAMEL PECAN ROLLS❧

Topping:
1 1/4 cups sifted powdered sugar
    1/2 cup whipping cream
        1 cup coarsely chopped pecans

Dough:
        2 - 14 to 16 oz. loaves frozen sweet roll or
            white bread dough, thawed

Filling:
        3 T. butter, melted
    1/2 cup packed brown sugar
        1 T. cinnamon
    3/4 cup raisins (opt.)

Preheat oven to 375 degrees.

For topping, in a small mixing bowl, stir together powdered sugar and whipping cream. Pour evenly into two 9-inch round baking pans. Sprinkle pecans over sugar mixture.

On a lightly floured surface, roll each loaf of dough into a 8x12-inch rectangle. Brush with melted butter. In a small mixing bowl, combine brown sugar and cinnamon; sprinkle over dough. If desired, top with raisins.

Roll up rectangle dough, jelly-roll style, starting from a long side. Pinch seam and ends to seal. Cut each roll into 10 to 12 slices. Place slices, seam sides down, on sugar mixture in pans. Cover with a towel. Let rise in a warm place until nearly double (about 30 minutes). (Or, cover with oiled waxed paper, then with plastic wrap. Refrigerate for 2 to 24 hours. Before baking, let chilled rolls stand, covered, 20 minutes at room temperature.)

Puncture surface bubbles with a greased toothpick before baking. Bake rolls, uncovered until golden brown, 20 to 25 minutes for unchilled rolls and 25 to 30 minutes for chilled rolls. To prevent burning, cover rolls with foil the last 10 minutes of baking. Cool in pans on a wire rack for 5 minutes. Invert onto serving plates.

CHERRY BERRY COFFEE CAKE

Filling:
    16 oz. can pitted cherries
    1 cup frozen cranberries
    1 cup sugar

Cake:
    8 oz. cream cheese, softened
    1/2 cup butter
1 1/2 cups sugar
    2 eggs
    1 tsp. almond extract
    1/4 cup milk
1 1/3 cups flour
    1 tsp. baking powder
    1/2 tsp. baking soda

Topping:
  nuts, sugar, and cinnamon (opt.)

Preheat oven to 350 degrees.

In a saucepan, combine the cherries and cranberries. Cook until the cranberries pop. Remove from heat and add the sugar. Cool.

For cake, in a medium mixing bowl, cream together the cream cheese, butter, and sugar. Add eggs, almond extract, and milk. Combine the flour, baking powder, and baking soda. Add to butter mixture; beat until thoroughly combined. Pour half the batter into a greased and floured 9x13-inch glass pan. Pour the filling over the batter in the baking dish, then cover with the remaining batter, dropping small amounts from a spoon.

Sprinkle nuts, sugar, and cinnamon over the top. Bake for 45 to 50 minutes, or until done.

CHERRY CINNAMON UPSIDE-DOWN COFFEE CAKE

Topping:
> 3 cups pitted fresh cherries
> > -OR-
>
> 3 cups frozen, thawed, drained sweet cherries
> > -OR-
>
> 24 oz. canned cherries, pitted
> 1/2 cup sugar

1 1/2 tsp. cinnamon
> 1/3 cup butter, softened

Cake:
> 2 cups flour
> 1/2 cup sugar
> 1 T. baking powder
> 1 tsp. salt
> 1/3 cup milk
> 1 egg
> 1/3 cup oil
> 1 tsp. vanilla

Preheat oven to 350 degrees.

Coat inside of a 9x13-inch pan with melted butter. For topping, combine cherries, sugar, cinnamon, and butter. Arrange mixture on bottom of pan.

Sift flour, sugar, baking powder, and salt into a large mixing bowl. Blend in milk, egg, oil, and vanilla. Beat at medium speed. Do not overbeat. Spread batter over cherry mixture.

Bake for 30 minutes. Turn cake upside down onto platter.

Another recipe from my mom.

CHOCOLATE CHIP SOUR CREAM STREUSEL COFFEE CAKE

Cake:
  3/4 cup butter, softened
1 1/2 cups sugar
    3 eggs
    2 tsp. vanilla
    3 cups flour
1 1/2 tsp. baking powder
1 1/2 tsp. baking soda
    1/2 tsp. salt
1 1/2 cups sour cream (may use light)
1 1/2 cups mini chocolate chips

Streusel Filling:
    1/4 cup light-brown sugar, packed
    1/4 cup walnuts, finely chopped (opt.)

Chocolate Glaze:
    2 T. sugar
    2 T. water
    1/2 cup chocolate chips, mini or regular

Preheat oven to 350 degrees.

In large mixing bowl, beat butter, sugar, eggs, and vanilla until light and fluffy. In separate bowl, sift together flour, baking powder, baking soda, and salt. Add dry ingredients to the butter mixture, alternating with sour cream. Stir in mini chocolate chips. Spread half of the batter into greased and floured 12-cup fluted tube pan.

In small bowl, stir together brown sugar, nuts, and cinnamon; sprinkle evenly over batter. Spread remaining batter evenly over top. Bake 55 to 60 minutes or until golden brown and toothpick inserted in cake comes out clean. Cool 15 minutes; remove from pan to wire rack. Cool completely.

For the glaze, in small saucepan, heat sugar and water to boiling, stirring until sugar dissolves. Remove from heat and immediately add mini chocolate chips. Stir until melted. Continue stirring to desired consistency and drizzle over the top of the cooled cake.

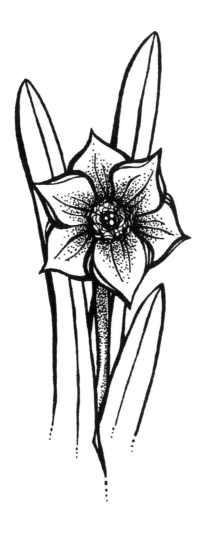

ൟCHOCOLATE CHIP SOUR CREAM COFFEE CAKE

Cake:
  1/2 cup butter, softened
    1 cup sugar
    2 eggs
    1 cup sour cream
    2 cups flour
    1 tsp. baking powder
  1/4 tsp. salt

Filling:
  1/2 cup sugar
    1 tsp. cinnamon
    6 oz. package chocolate chips (about 1 cup)
  1/2 cup chopped nuts (opt.)

Preheat oven to 350 degrees.

To make the batter, beat together the butter and sugar. Add the eggs one at a time, then sour cream. Sift together the flour, baking powder, and salt. Add to the egg mixture and beat until throroughly combined. Spoon half the batter into a greased and floured tube pan.

For the filling, combine the sugar, cinnamon, chocolate chips, and nuts. Spread half the filling over the batter. With a knife, cut through the batter to swirl. Add the rest of the batter, then top with the rest of the filling. Again cut through the batter to swirl. Bake for 45 minutes, or until done.

❧CHOCOLATE ZUCCHINI CAKE❧

Cake:
  1/2 cup butter, softened
  1/2 cup oil
1 3/4 cup sugar
    2 eggs
    1 tsp. vanilla
  1/2 cup sour milk
2 1/2 cups flour
    4 T. cocoa
    1 tsp. baking soda
  1/2 tsp. cinnamon
  1/2 tsp. cloves
  1/2 tsp. salt
    2 cups finely diced zucchini

Topping:
  1/4 cup semisweet chocolate pieces
  1/4 cup chopped nuts (opt.)

Preheat oven to 325 degrees.

Cream butter, oil, and sugar together. Add eggs, vanilla, and sour milk. Blend thoroughly. Sift together flour, cocoa, baking soda, cinnamon, cloves and salt. Blend with creamed mixture. Stir in zucchini. Spoon into greased and floured 9x13-inch pan. Sprinkle with chocolate pieces and nuts. Bake 45 minutes or until done.

NOTE: If you don't happen to have any sour milk in your refrigerator, add 1 1/2 teaspoons vinegar to 1/2 cup milk.

This is a delicious cake, suitable for pot lucks, picnics, or breakfast. The zucchini is almost invisible, certainly tasteless, but gives it a wonderful moistness. ...Chocolatey, yet not too sweet.

✖CINNAMON COFFEE CAKE✖

Cake:
- 1 cup butter, softened
- 2 cups sugar
- 2 tsp. vanilla
- 4 eggs
- 3 cups flour
- 2 tsp. baking powder
- 1 tsp. baking soda
- 1/2 tsp. salt
- 2 cups sour cream

Filling/Topping:
- 3/4 cup sugar
- 2 tsp. cinnamon
- 1/2 cup chopped walnuts (opt.)

Preheat oven to 350 degrees.

For cake, in a large mixing bowl, cream together butter and sugar until light and fluffy. Add vanilla. Add eggs, one at a time, beating well after each addition. In separate bowl combine flour, baking powder, baking soda, and salt; add alternately with sour cream, beating just enough after each addition to keep batter smooth. Spoon one-third of batter into a greased 10-inch tube pan.

For filling/topping, combine sugar, cinnamon, nuts; sprinkle one-third over batter in pan. Repeat layers two more times.

Bake for 70 minutes or until cake tests done. Cool 10 minutes. Remove from pan to a wire rack to cool completely.

Light and airy – sweet enough.

CINNAMON RAISIN COFFEE CAKE

Cake:
1 1/2 cups flour
   1 T. baking powder
  1/4 tsp. salt
  3/4 cup sugar
  1/4 cup butter, softened
   1 egg, lightly beaten
  1/2 cup milk
   1 tsp. vanilla

Filling:
  1/2 cup brown sugar, firmly packed
   2 T. flour
   2 tsp. cinnamon
  1/2 cup raisins or chopped walnuts (opt.)
   2 T. butter, melted

Preheat oven to 375 degrees.

Combine flour, baking powder, salt, and sugar; cut in butter with a pastry blender until blended. Combine egg, milk, and vanilla; add to flour mixture, stirring until blended. Spoon two-thirds of batter into a greased and floured 9-inch round cake pan.

For filling, combine brown sugar, flour, cinnamon, and raisins or walnuts; stir in butter. Sprinkle this mixture over the batter in the pan, and top with remaining batter. Bake for 25 minutes or until done.

❧CINNAMON SWIRL COFFEE CAKE❧

Cake:
    3 cups flour
1 1/2 cup sugar
    2 tsp. baking powder
    1 tsp. baking soda
    1 tsp. salt
    1 cup buttermilk
    3/4 cup butter, softened
    3 eggs
    2 T. orange juice
    1 T. grated orange peel
    1/4 cup raisins (opt.)

Filling:
    1/2 cup brown sugar, firmly packed
    1/3 cup flour
    2 tsp. cinnamon
    1/4 cup butter

Glaze:
    1 cup confectioner's sugar
1 to 2 T. orange juice

Preheat oven to 350 degrees.

For cake, in a large mixing bowl, blend flour, sugar, baking powder, baking soda, and salt. Add buttermilk, butter, eggs, orange juice, and orange peel. Beat at least 2 minutes at medium speed. Stir in the raisins. Pour one-third of the batter into a greased fluted tube pan.

For the filling, in a small mixing bowl, mix the brown sugar, flour, cinnamon, and butter until crumbly. Sprinkle half of the mixture over batter in the pan. Pour another one-third of the batter into the pan. Sprinkle with the remaining filling mixture and top with the remaining batter. Bake for 50 to 60 minutes or until a toothpick inserted in the center comes out clean. Cool upright in the pan 15 minutes; turn onto a serving plate.

For the glaze, in a small bowl, stir the confectioner's sugar and 1 to 2 tablespoons of orange juice together. Drizzle over the cake.

Light, with a delicate citrus flavor and plenty of cinnamon.

❧COCONUT COFFEE CAKE❧

Cake:
   1 box yellow cake mix
   1 can condensed Cheddar cheese soup
1/2 cup water
   2 eggs
   1 T. grated lemon rind
   1 cup shredded coconut
1/2 cup crushed pineapple, drained
1/2 cup chopped nuts (opt.)

Topping:
   3 T. butter, softened
1/2 cup flour
1/4 cup brown sugar, firmly packed
1/2 cup shredded coconut

Preheat oven to 350 degrees.

For cake, in a large mixing bowl, combine the cake mix, soup, water, eggs, and lemon rind. Beat until well blended. Stir in coconut, pineapple, and nuts. Spread the batter evenly in a greased and floured 9x13-inch pan.

For topping, in another bowl, using pastry blender or 2 knives, cut butter into the flour until crumbly. Stir in brown sugar and coconut. Sprinkle over the batter. Bake for 45-50 minutes or until done.

Don't let the soup scare you - it is undetectable! This cake is very moist, and if you like coconut, you'll love this one!

৵COFFEE CAKE CRUNCH৵

Cake:
    1/3 cup butter
    3/4 cup sugar
      1 egg
1 1/2 cups sifted flour
    2 tsp. baking powder
    1/2 tsp. salt
    1/2 cup milk

Topping:
    4 T. butter, melted
    1/2 cup light-brown sugar, firmly packed
    2 T. flour
    2 tsp. cinnamon
    1/2 cup chopped nuts (opt.)

Preheat oven to 375 degrees.

In large bowl, beat butter and sugar together until creamy; add egg and beat thoroughly. Sift together flour, baking powder, and salt. Add flour mixture to butter mixture alternately with milk; beat well after each addition. Pour into greased 9-inch round pan.

For topping, combine butter, brown sugar, flour, cinnamon, and nuts. Sprinkle over batter. Bake 30 to 35 minutes, or until tests done. Serve warm.

∽COFFEE CAKE with Jam∾

Cake:
   1/3 cup shortening or butter, softened
   3/4 cup sugar
     1 egg
1 1/2 cups flour
    2 tsp. baking powder
   1/2 tsp. salt
   1/2 cup milk

Topping:
   1/3 cup jam (raspberry, apricot, strawberry, cherry, or...)
    2 T. sugar
   1/4 tsp. cinnamon
   1/4 tsp. nutmeg
    1 T. butter, softened

Preheat oven to 375 degrees.

For cake, beat shortening (or butter) and sugar together until creamy; add egg and beat thoroughly. Sift together flour, baking powder, and salt. Add to creamed mixture alternately with milk; beat well after each addition. Pour into a greased and floured 9-inch round cake pan.

For topping, stir jam with a fork until smooth. Drop by teaspoonfuls over batter. With a knife, cut through the batter several times to marble. Combine sugar, cinnamon, nutmeg, and butter. Sprinkle over batter. Bake 30 to 35 minutes, or until tests done. Serve warm.

❧COFFEE CAKE❧

Cake:
  1/4 cup butter, softened
    1 cup sugar
    2 egg yolks, well-beaten
    2 cups flour
    2 tsp. baking powder
    1 tsp. salt
    1 cup milk
    2 egg whites, beaten

Filling/Topping:
1 1/2 cup brown sugar, firmly packed
    2 T. flour
    2 T. melted butter
    2 tsp. cinnamon
    1 cup nuts (opt.)

Preheat oven to 350 degrees.

For the cake, in a medium mixing bowl cream butter; add the sugar gradually. Add the egg yolks. In a separate bowl sift together flour, baking powder, and salt, and add alternately with the milk to the butter mixture. Add the beaten egg whites. Pour half the batter into a greased 9x13-inch baking pan.

For the filling/topping, mix together the brown sugar, flour, butter, cinnamon, and nuts.

Spread half of the filling/topping over the batter in pan. Pour the remaining batter over and top with the rest of the filling/topping. Bake about 30 minutes or until tests done.

This is a basic coffee cake, however, the amount of brown sugar makes it quite sweet!

❧COFFEE COFFEE CAKE❧

Cake:
   2 cups sifted flour
   1 cup sugar
   1 T. baking powder
   2 tsp. instant coffee
1/2 tsp. salt
   3 T. butter, melted
   1 cup milk
   1 egg, beaten
   1 tsp. vanilla

Topping:
1/2 cup crushed corn flakes
   2 T. sugar
1/2 tsp. cinnamon
   2 T. butter, melted

Preheat oven to 350 degrees.

For the cake, sift flour, sugar, baking powder, coffee, and salt. Combine melted butter, milk, egg, and vanilla. Stir into dry ingredients. Turn into greased 8-inch square pan.

For topping, combine corn flakes, sugar, cinnamon, and butter. Scatter over batter. Bake for 45 minutes or until done.

My sister, Eileen Bonn Spencer, gave me this recipe twenty-some years ago. It has become our family favorite.

❧COFFEE KUCHEN❧

Cake:
    3 cups sifted flour
    3 tsp. baking powder
  1/2 tsp. salt
1 1/4 tsp. cinnamon
    1 cup sugar
    1 cup light-brown sugar, firmly packed
    3 T. instant coffee
  1/2 cup butter
  1/2 cup shortening
    1 cup milk
  1/8 tsp. baking soda
    2 eggs, slightly beaten

Topping:
    1 cup of first 9 ingredients

Preheat oven to 350 degrees.

In a large bowl, sift flour with baking powder, salt, cinnamon, sugar, brown sugar, and coffee. Using pastry blender or 2 knives, cut butter and shortening into flour mixture until it resembles course crumbs. **Set aside 1 cup for topping.**

Mix together milk, baking soda, and eggs. Pour egg mixture into flour mixture; stir with a wooden spoon, just until combined. Spread into lightly greased and floured 9-inch tube pan. Sprinkle with reserved topping mixture.

Bake 55 to 60 minutes, or until toothpick inserted into center comes out clean. Place pan on wire rack 10 minutes. Remove from pan. Serve warm.

This has a very distinct coffee flavor. Great cake – best eaten warm.

CRANBERRY APPLE COFFEE CAKE WREATH

Cake:
1 1/3 cups flour
   1 cup whole wheat flour
   2 tsp. baking soda
   2 tsp. cinnamon
1 1/2 cups sugar
   1/4 tsp. salt
   4 egg whites
   1/2 cup applesauce, preferably chunky
   3 large tart apples, (Pippin or Granny Smith), peeled, cored
      and cut into small chunks (about 3 cups)
   1 cup cranberries, fresh or frozen

Topping:
   1/4 cup sugar
   1/2 cup light brown sugar, firmly packed
      dash salt
   1/4 cup plain yogurt (regular, low-fat, or nonfat fine)
1 1/2 cups pecan halves (opt.)
   1 small red apple, unpeeled, cut into 1/4-inch slices
   1 small green apple, unpeeled, cut into 1/4-inch slices
   1/3 cup cranberries, fresh or frozen

Preheat oven to 350 degrees.

For the cake, in large bowl and using electric mixer, combine flour, whole wheat flour, baking soda, cinnamon, sugar, and salt; mix thoroughly; add egg whites and applesauce. Mix until batter is moistened. Add chopped apples and cranberries; mix thoroughly.

Pour batter into a greased 12-inch tube pan with removable bottom (such as angel food cake pan). It will fill only about one third of the pan. Bake for 45 to 55 minutes, or until toothpick inserted in center comes out clean. Cool in pan 10 minutes. Cake will fall as it cools. Go around edges with a knife and remove sides of pan. Cut away from bottom and invert onto rack. Cool completely. (Cake may be refrigerated up to 2 days or frozen.)

To make topping, up to two hours before serving, in a large or 3-quart microwave-safe bowl, stir sugar, brown sugar, salt, and yogurt together until blended. Microwave, uncovered, on high (100%) for 5 to 7 minutes without stirring, until caramel color. Stir in pecans, apple slices, and cranberries. Microwave on high (100%) for 1 to 3 minutes, or until caramel is melted and syrupy. Stir fruit to coat. With a slotted spoon, remove fruit and nuts and spoon over top of cake. Set caramel aside until it thickens enough to coat. Spoon over fruit. (If caramel gets too thick, microwave for a few seconds.)

❧COWBOY COFFEE CAKE❧

Cake:
1 1/2 cups flour
   1 cup brown sugar, firmly packed
  1/3 cup butter
   1 tsp. baking powder
  1/4 tsp. baking soda
  1/4 tsp. cinnamon
  1/4 tsp. nutmeg
  1/2 cup buttermilk
   1 egg, beaten

Topping:
  1/2 cup first 3 ingredients

Preheat oven to 375 degrees.

In a mixing bowl, stir together flour and brown sugar. Cut in butter until mixture resembles fine crumbs. **Set aside 1/2 cup of the crumb mixture for topping**. To remaining crumb mixture, add baking powder, baking soda, cinnamon, and nutmeg; mix well. Add buttermilk and egg; mix well. Pour into a greased 8x8-inch pan.

Sprinkle reserved crumb mixture over the top of the batter. Bake for about 25 minutes or until a wooden toothpick inserted near center comes out clean. Serve warm.

So simple, yet so good -- a pretty darn fancy "Home on the Range" breakfast.

CRANBERRY COCONUT COFFEE CAKE

Cake:
- 1 package yellow cake mix
- 1 3.4 oz. package vanilla instant pudding mix
- 5 eggs

1/2 cup oil
1/2 cup bourbon
1/2 cup milk
- 2 cups fresh or frozen cranberries, thawed and chopped
- 1 cup chopped pecans (opt.)
- 1 cup flaked coconut

Topping:
- Powdered sugar

Preheat oven to 350 degrees.

For cake, in a large mixing bowl, combine cake mix, pudding mix, eggs, oil, bourbon, and milk. With an electric mixer, beat at low speed until smooth; beat at high speed 3 minutes. Fold in cranberries, pecans, and coconut. Pour mixture into a greased and floured bundt pan.

Bake for 55 minutes or until a toothpick inserted in center of cake comes out clean. Cool in pan on a wire rack 10 minutes; remove from pan, invert and let cool completely on wire rack. Using sifter, sprinkle with powdered sugar.

"Out of this world," "great crustiness," describes this cake. The bourbon-soaked cranberries are really tasty!

CRANBERRY COFFEE CAKE
with Butter Cream Sauce

Cake:
 2 T. butter
 1 cup sugar
 1 tsp. vanilla
 2 cups flour
 1 T. baking powder
1/4 tsp. salt
 1 cup milk
 2 cups cranberries

Sauce:
1/2 cup butter
 1 cup sugar
1/2 cup light cream

Preheat oven to 375 degrees.

For cake, cream the butter and sugar together; add vanilla. Sift together the flour, baking powder, and salt; add alternately with the milk to the butter mixture. Fold in the cranberries and pour into a greased and floured 9x13-inch pan. Bake 35 minutes or until done.

Meanwhile, for the sauce, in a small saucepan stir together the butter, sugar, and cream over medium heat until mixture boils. Continue stirring and boil three minutes. Pour over hot coffee cake straight out of the oven. Serve immediately.

CRANBERRY NUT COFFEE CAKE

Cake:
- 1/4 cup butter, softened
- 1/2 cup sugar
- 1 egg
- 2/3 cup milk
- 1/2 tsp. vanilla
- 1 1/2 cups sifted flour
- 1/8 tsp. salt
- 2 tsp. baking powder

Topping:
- 1/4 cup brown sugar
- 1/2 cup chopped nuts (opt.)
- 1/4 tsp. cinnamon
- 2/3 cup cranberry pulp

Icing:
- 1 cup confectioner's sugar
- 1/2 tsp. vanilla
- 1 T. water

Preheat oven to 400 degrees.

For the cake, in a large mixing bowl, cream the butter and sugar until light and fluffy. Beat in the egg, milk, and vanilla. Combine the flour, salt, and baking powder; add to butter mixture and beat well. Pour into a greased 9-inch square pan.

For topping, in a small bowl, combine the brown sugar, nuts, and cinnamon. Sprinkle over the batter. Spoon the cranberry pulp over the top. Bake for 20 to 25 minutes.

For icing, combine confectioner's sugar, vanilla, and water. Drizzle over cake while it is still warm.

CRANBERRY SWIRL COFFEE CAKE

Cake:
1/4 cup butter, softened
   1 cup sugar
   2 eggs, well beaten
   1 tsp. almond extract
   2 cups flour
   1 tsp. baking soda
1/4 tsp. salt
   1 cup sour cream

Filling/Topping:
   8 oz. whole cranberry sauce
1/2 cup chopped walnuts (opt.)

Preheat oven to 350 degrees.

For cake, cream the butter and sugar together; add the eggs, beat well; add almond extract. Mix together the flour, baking soda, and salt; add to butter mixture alternately with sour cream. Pour half the batter into a greased tube pan.

For filling/topping, stir the cranberry sauce in a small bowl, then spoon half of the cranberry sauce over batter, cutting it into the batter in a swirling motion. Sprinkle half of the walnuts over the sauce, then repeat layers. Bake for 55 to 60 minutes, or until done.

CRANBERRY WALNUT COFFEE CAKE

Cake:
1/2 cup butter, softened
　1 cup sugar
　2 eggs
　1 cup plain yogurt
　2 cups flour
　1 tsp. baking powder
　2 tsp. baking soda
　1 cup fresh cranberries, chopped
　1 cup walnuts, chopped

Topping:
1/2 cup flour
1/4 cup sugar
1/4 cup butter
　1 cup fresh cranberries, chopped

Preheat oven to 375 degrees.

For cake, cream butter and sugar until light and fluffy. Beat in eggs. Add yogurt. In separate bowl combine flour, baking powder, and baking soda. Stir into creamed mixture until just combined. Do not over mix. Gently fold in chopped cranberries and the nuts. Pour into a greased 9x13-inch pan.

For topping, combine flour and sugar. Cut in butter using pastry blender or two knives until crumbly. Sprinkle the remaining cranberries over the top of the batter .

Bake for 25-30 minutes until tests done.

CREAM CHEESE PASTRY with Jam

1 cup prepared biscuit mix
2 oz. cream cheese
2 T. butter
3 T. milk
1/4 cup jam (raspberry or whatever other jam you like)

Preheat oven to 400.

Measure biscuit mix into large mixing bowl. Cut in cream cheese and butter to dry mix using pastry blender. Should be small crumbs. Stir in milk, 1 tablespoon at a time, using a fork until the dough clings together in a ball; not too sticky.

Knead on lightly floured board 10 to 15 times, until smooth. Roll out into even rectangle. Spread jam down center of dough.

Cut slits along both sides of dough 1 inch apart. Fold strips over jam. Put on ungreased cookie sheet. Bake 10 to 15 minutes.

My son, Carey Bonn, brought this recipe home and has made it many times himself. It's simple, and really good.

CREAM CHEESE RASPBERRY COFFEE CAKE

Cake:
- 8 oz. cream cheese
- 1 cup sugar
- 1/2 cup butter, softened
- 2 eggs
- 1/4 cup milk
- 1/2 tsp. vanilla
- 1 3/4 cups flour
- 1 tsp. baking powder
- 1/2 tsp. baking soda
- 1/8 tsp. salt
- 1/2 cup seedless raspberry preserves (strawberry or blackberry fine)

Topping:
Sifted powdered sugar

Preheat oven to 350 degrees.

In a large mixing bowl of an electric mixer, beat cream cheese, sugar, and butter on medium speed until light and fluffy. Add eggs, milk, and vanilla. Stir together the flour, baking powder, baking soda, and salt; slowly add to the creamed mixture. Beat for about 2 minutes or until well mixed.

Spread batter evenly in a greased and floured 13x9-inch baking pan. Spoon preserves in 8 to 10 portions on top of batter. With a knife, swirl preserves into batter to marble.

Bake for 30 to 35 minutes or until toothpick comes out clean. Cool slightly on a wire rack. Sift powdered sugar over the top of the cake. Serve warm.

❧DANISH APPLE COCONUT COFFEE CAKE❧

Cake:
 3/4 cup butter, softened
 1 cup sugar
 3 eggs
1 1/2 cup sifted flour
 2 tsp. baking powder
 1/4 tsp. salt
 1/2 cup milk
1 1/4 cups coconut, shredded
 2 large tart apples, peeled and diced

Topping:
 1/4 cup sliced almonds
 2 T. sugar

Preheat oven to 350 degrees.

For the cake, cream together butter and sugar until smooth; add eggs, blending thoroughly. Sift flour again with the baking powder and salt, adding it to the creamed mixture alternately with the milk, blending until smooth. Stir in the coconut, then fold in the apples. Pour into a well-greased 9x13-inch pan.

For topping, sprinkle with the almonds, then with sugar. Bake for 30 to 35 minutes, or until cake tests done.

This is a light cakes that could be used for desert, potluck, or picnic. The coconut and apple combined make it moist with a hint of tropics.

❧DATE COFFEE CAKE❧

Cake:
- 2 cups flour
- 1/2 cup sugar
- 2 tsp. baking powder
- 1/4 tsp. baking soda
- 1 tsp. cinnamon
- 1/8 tsp. nutmeg
- 1 cup sour cream
- 1/4 cup oil
- 2 eggs, lightly beaten
- 1 1/2 cup chopped dates

Topping:
- 2 T. sugar
- 1/4 tsp. cinnamon
- 1/4 cup finely chopped walnuts (opt.)

Preheat oven to 350 degrees.

For the cake, in a large bowl, combine flour, sugar, baking powder, baking soda, cinnamon, and nutmeg.

In a separate bowl, stir together sour cream, oil, and eggs; stir into dry ingredients just until blended; stir in chopped dates. Spread batter in lightly greased 9-inch round springform pan or 9x9-inch square pan.

For topping, combine, sugar, cinnamon, and walnuts. Sprinkle over cake. Bake 40 to 45 minutes or until toothpick inserted in center comes out clean. Remove springform ring. Serve warm.

❧DRIED FRUIT COFFEE CAKE❧

Cake:
   3/4 cup butter
1 1/2 cups sugar
   2 eggs
   1 tsp. vanilla
2 1/4 cups flour
   2 tsp. baking powder
   1/2 tsp. baking soda
   1/2 tsp. salt
   1 cup sour cream
   1/4 cup chopped walnuts
   1/4 cup dried chopped dates
   1/4 cup chopped prunes
   1/4 cup dried chopped apricots

Topping:
   1/2 tsp. cinnamon
   2 T. sugar

Preheat oven to 350 degrees.

For cake, cream together the butter and sugar; add the eggs and beat until light and fluffy; add vanilla. Combine flour, baking powder, baking soda, and salt. Add half the dry ingredients to butter mixture; add sour cream and beat until smooth. Beat in the remaining flour mixture. Stir in walnuts and fruit. Spread the batter in a greased and floured 10-inch tube pan.

For topping, combine cinnamon and sugar, and sprinkle over the batter. Bake for 45 minutes or until done.

❧EGGNOG COFFEE CAKE❧

Cake:
     1/2 cup butter
1 1/3 cup sugar
          2 eggs
      3 cups flour
      1 T. baking powder
      2 cups eggnog

Glaze:
1 1/2 cup powdered sugar
   2-3 T. eggnog
          nutmeg

Preheat oven to 350 degrees.

For the cake, cream together butter and sugar. Beat in eggs. Mix together flour and baking powder, and stir into creamed mixture alternately with the eggnog.

Pour into a greased and floured 9x13-inch pan. Bake for 45 to 60 minutes or until toothpick inserted into thickest part comes out clean.

For glaze, combine powdered sugar with just enough eggnog to make it drizzling consistency. Pour over cake and sprinkle lightly with nutmeg.

Nice, light eggnog flavor - great for the holidays.

❧ELECTRIC SKILLET SOUR CREAM COFFEE CAKE ❧

Cake:
1 1/2 cups flour
   1 cup sugar
   2 tsp. baking powder
   1/2 tsp. baking soda
   1/2 tsp. salt
   1 cup sour cream
   2 eggs, beaten

Topping:
   1/2 cup brown sugar
   2 T. flour
1 1/2 tsp. cinnamon
   2 T. butter, melted
   1/2 cup chopped nuts, pecans are nice (opt.)

Heat electric skillet (12-inch round or whatever you have) to 280 degrees. Grease and flour, or use pan coating spray on Teflon skillets.

Mix together flour, sugar, baking powder, baking soda, and salt. Combine sour cream and beaten eggs; mix thoroughly. Add dry ingredients to sour cream mixture; mix thoroughly. Spread batter into heated skillet; cover. Bake 25 minutes or until top is dry. The top will not brown, but the bottom will.

Meanwhile, for topping, work together brown sugar, flour, cinnamon, and butter. Add nuts. When cake is done, sprinkle topping over top. With paper towel, wipe condensation from the inside of the lid and replace lid on skillet. **Turn off skillet.** Let stand with lid on for 10 minutes.

My childhood friend, Sheryl Looney Selee, says this recipe has been in her family her whole life. This cake kind of reminds me of sweet cinnamon biscuits or rolls.

⧗EVERYDAY COFFEE CAKE⧗

Cake:
    1 egg
    3/4 cup sugar
    1/3 cup butter, melted
    1/2 cup milk
    1 tsp. vanilla
1 1/2 cups sifted flour
2 1/2 tsp. baking powder
    1/2 tsp. salt

Topping:
    2 T. sugar
    1 tsp. cinnamon

Preheat oven to 375 degrees.

For cake, in medium bowl, beat egg until frothy; add sugar and butter until well combined; add milk and vanilla. Sift together flour, baking powder, and salt. With wooden spoon, add flour mixture to butter mixture until well combined. Pour into greased 8x8-inch pan or 9-inch round pan.

For topping, combine sugar and cinnamon. Sprinkle over top of batter. Bake 25 to 30 minutes, or until toothpick inserted into center of cake comes out clean. Serve warm.

Note: For **crumb topping**, combine 1/2 cup sugar, 1/4 cup flour, 1/4 cup soft butter, and 1 tsp. cinnamon. Mix with fork until crumbly. Use in place of sugar/cinnamon topping, above.

Quick and easy, light and breezy...

✌FRESH APPLE COFFEE CAKE✌

    4 cups peeled, diced apples
    2 cups sugar
    1 cup chopped nuts (opt.)
    3 cups flour
1/2 tsp. nutmeg
    1 tsp. cinnamon
    2 tsp. baking soda
1/2 tsp. salt
    1 cup cooking oil
    1 tsp. vanilla
    2 eggs, well beaten

Preheat oven to 350 degrees.

Mix together the apples, sugar, and nuts in a mixing bowl; let stand for 1 hour, stirring often.

Mix together the flour, nutmeg, cinnamon, baking soda, and salt; add to the apples, mixing well. Then add the oil, vanilla, and eggs; mix well. Pour the batter into a greased and floured tube pan and bake for 1 hour, or until tests done.

❧GERMAN COFFEE CAKE❧

Cake:
1/2 cup butter
  1 cup sugar
  2 eggs
  1 cup sour cream
  1 tsp. vanilla
  2 cups flour
  1 tsp. baking soda
  1 tsp. baking powder
1/2 tsp. salt

Topping:
1/4 cup sugar
1/2 cup chopped nuts (opt.)
  1 tsp. cinnamon

Preheat oven to 350 degrees.

For cake, cream butter and sugar thoroughly. Add eggs, sour cream, and vanilla. Mix together flour, baking soda, baking powder, and salt; add to creamed mixture. Beat well. Pour into a 9x13-inch greased pan.

For topping, combine sugar, nuts, and cinnamon. Sprinkle the topping over the cake and marbleize by lightly cutting the topping into the batter with a knife. Bake for 35 to 40 minutes, or until done.

❧FRESH BLUEBERRY COFFEE CAKE❧

Filling/Topping:
1 1/4 cups fresh blueberries
    1/3 cup sugar
      2 T. flour

Cake:
    1/2 cup butter, softened
      1 cup sugar
      2 eggs
      1 tsp. vanilla or almond extract
      2 cups flour
      1 tsp. baking powder
    1/2 tsp. salt
      8 oz. sour cream
    1/2 cup chopped pecans (opt.)

Glaze:
    3/4 cup sifted powdered sugar
      1 T. warm water
      1 tsp. vanilla or almond extract

Preheat oven to 350 degrees.

For filling/topping, combine blueberries, sugar, and flour in a small saucepan; cook over medium heat 5 minutes or until thickened, stirring constantly. Cool (may refrigerate).

For cake, cream butter; gradually add sugar, thoroughly mix using medium speed of an electric mixer. Add eggs, one at a time, beating after each addition; add vanilla. Combine flour, baking powder, and salt; add to creamed mixture alternately with sour cream, beginning and ending with flour mixture.

Spoon half of batter into a heavily greased 10-inch tube pan. Spoon half the blueberry mixture over batter. Repeat with remaining batter and blueberry mixture. Swirl through batter with a knife. Sprinkle pecans over the top. Bake at 350 for 50 minutes or until done. Let cool in pan 10 minutes; invert to a serving plate.

For glaze, combine powdered sugar, water and extract in a small bowl. Stir with a fork until smooth. Drizzle over warm coffee cake.

Such a delicious coffee cake, it's hard to stop at one piece! The bottom of this cake is prettier than the top, so I don't invert it.

GRAHAM STREUSEL COFFEE CAKE

Cake:
>   1 package yellow or white cake mix
>   1 cup water
>   1/4 cup oil
>   3 eggs

Streusel:
1 1/2 cups graham cracker crumbs
>   (about 21 crackers)
>   3/4 cup chopped pecans or walnuts (opt.)
>   3/4 cup packed brown sugar
1 1/2 tsp. cinnamon
>   2/3 cup butter, melted

Icing:
>   1 cup powdered sugar
>   1 tsp. vanilla
>   water

Preheat oven to 350 degrees.

For cake, in a large mixing bowl, combine cake mix, water, oil, and eggs. Beat on low speed of an electric mixer until moistened, then beat on medium speed for 1 to 2 minutes. Pour half of the batter into a greased 9x13-inch baking pan.

For streusel, in a medium mixing bowl combine graham cracker crumbs, pecans or walnuts, brown sugar, and cinnamon. Stir in the melted butter. Sprinkle batter with half of the streusel. Carefully spread the remaining batter over streusel; sprinkle with remaining streusel.

Bake for 35 to 40 minutes or until a toothpick inserted near the center comes out clean. Cool slightly.

For the icing, stir together in a small bowl, the powdered sugar, vanilla, and enough water to make drizzling consistency. Drizzle icing over the top of the warm cake. Serve warm.

Exceptionally good, <u>very</u> sweet...could leave off the icing and it would still be great!

☙JELLY COFFEE CAKE☙

Cake:
    1/4 cup butter, softened
    1/3 cup sugar
      1 egg
      1 tsp. vanilla
      1 cup flour
1 1/2 tsp. baking powder
        dash salt
    1/3 cup milk
    1/3 cup jelly

Topping:
    2 T. butter
    2 T. sugar
    1/2 tsp. cinnamon
    1/4 cup flour

For cake, cream together butter and sugar. Add the egg and vanilla. Combine flour, baking powder, and salt. Add to butter mixture alternately with milk. Pour the batter into a well-greased 8-inch pan. Dot with jelly.

For topping, combine butter, sugar, cinnamon, and flour until crumbly. Sprinkle over batter. Bake for 30 minutes, or until tests done.

⮞LEMON POPPY SEED COFFEE CAKE⮜

        1/2 cup poppy seeds
        1/2 cup milk
1 1/2 cups butter
1 1/4 cups sugar
        2 T. grated lemon rind
        1 T. grated orange rind
        8 egg yolks
        2 cups cake flour (or all-purpose flour minus 2 tablespoons)
        1/2 tsp. salt

        3/4 tsp. cream of tartar
        1/8 tsp. salt
        8 egg whites
        1/4 cup sugar

Preheat oven to 350 degrees.

Soak the poppy seeds in milk for 4 hours.

In a large mixing bowl, cream the butter and sugar. Add the
lemon and orange rinds and the egg yolks. Add the flour and salt.
Beat for 5 minutes. Add the poppy seeds and milk. Mix well.

In a separate mixing bowl beat the cream of tartar and salt with
the egg whites. Beat until stiff, gradually adding sugar. Fold into
the poppy seed mixture and pour the batter into 2 greased and
floured 8x8-inch baking pans or a 9x13-inch pan. Bake for 40 to
60 minutes, or until done.

❧LEMON BALL COFFEE CAKE☙

Cake:
3 1/2 cups prepared buttermilk biscuit mix
1/4 cup light-brown sugar, firmly packed
1/4 sugar
1 tsp. cinnamon
1/2 tsp. nutmeg
2 T. butter, melted
1/2 cup milk
1 egg, slightly beaten

4 T. butter, melted

Topping:
1/4 cup slivered toasted almonds
3 T. light-brown sugar
1 T. grated lemon peel

Preheat oven to 350 degrees.

In large bowl, stir together biscuit mix, brown sugar, sugar, cinnamon, and nutmeg. Combine butter with milk and egg. Make a well in center of dry ingredients; add butter mixture all at once. Using a fork, stir only until dry ingredients are moistened. Shape dough into balls the size of walnuts.

Roll balls in 4 T. melted butter. Arrange 2 rows of balls in a buttered 9-inch tube pan with removable bottom (like an angel food cake pan).

For topping, combine almonds, brown sugar, and lemon peel. Sprinkle half this mixture over balls in the pan. Arrange remaining balls over the first layer, starting at the center of the pan. Sprinkle remaining topping over balls.

Bake 35 to 40 minutes, until lightly browned. Cool slightly. Cut around edges with a spatula and lift cake and bottom of pan to a flat tray. Separate balls with a fork. Serve warm.

❧LEMON WALNUT COFFEE CAKE❧

Cake:
   2 cups biscuit mix
1/2 cup chopped walnuts (opt.)
   1 egg, slightly beaten
1/2 cup milk
1/2 cup brown sugar, firmly packed
   3 T. butter, melted
   1 T. lemon juice
   2 tsp. grated lemon peel

Topping:
1/2 cup chopped walnuts (opt.)
   1 cup crushed corn flakes
1/4 cup sugar
1/2 tsp. cinnamon
   2 T. melted butter

Preheat oven to 375 degrees.

For cake, in a medium bowl, combine biscuit mix and walnuts. Combine egg, milk, brown sugar, and melted butter. Add to mix, and stir just until moistened; stir in lemon juice and peel. Pour into a greased 8-inch or 9-inch square pan.

For topping, combine walnuts, crushed corn flakes, sugar, cinnamon, and melted butter; mix until crumbly. Sprinkle topping over batter. Bake for 30 minutes or until golden brown and tests done.

❧MINCEMEAT BRUNCH CAKE☙

Cake:
  1 cup butter, softened
1 1/2 cups sugar
1 1/2 tsp. vanilla
  1/2 tsp. grated orange peel
    4 eggs
    3 cups flour
1 1/2 tsp. baking powder
    2 cup mincemeat
    2/3 cup chopped walnuts (opt.)

Glaze:
    1 cup confectioner's sugar
    2 T. orange juice

Preheat oven to 350 degrees.

For cake, cream together the butter and sugar; add the vanilla and orange peel. Add the eggs, one at a time, beating well after each addition. Mix together flour and baking powder; slowly add to butter mixture. Spread 2/3 of the batter into a 10x15-inch greased jelly-roll pan.

Spread mincemeat on top of batter. Drop remaining batter by the spoonful onto the mincemeat; about 15 drops. Sprinkle chopped walnuts over the top. Bake for 35 to 40 minutes, or until a toothpick inserted in the center comes out clean.

For glaze, using a fork, stir together the confectioner's sugar and orange juice. Drizzle over the warm cake.

～MOCHA SWIRL COFFEE CAKE～

Cake:
    1 cup butter, softened
1 3/4 cups sugar
2 1/2 tsp. vanilla
3 1/3 cups flour
3 1/4 tsp. baking powder
    1/2 tsp. salt
1 1/3 cups milk
    4 egg whites

Filling:
    1/2 cup sugar
    3 T. cocoa powder, unsweetened
    2 tsp. instant coffee powder
    1 tsp. cinnamon
    3 T. butter, chilled
        powdered sugar

Preheat oven to 350 degrees.

For cake, in a large mixing bowl at medium speed, beat butter and sugar until light and fluffy; add vanilla. Sift together flour, baking powder, and salt. Add to butter mixture, alternating with milk, starting and ending with flour mixture. In a small mixing bowl at high speed, beat egg whites until soft peaks form. Fold into batter. Spread one-third of the batter in greased 12-cup fluted tube pan.

For filling, combine sugar, cocoa powder, coffee powder, and cinnamon. Cut in butter with a pastry blender until crumbly. Sprinkle half the filling over the batter in the pan. Top with one-third of the batter; sprinkle with remaining filling mixture and top with remaining batter. With a knife, gently cut through batter to swirl.

Bake for 50 to 60 minutes, or until done. Cool for 15 minutes on a wire rack. Remove from pan and cool completely. Sprinkle with powdered sugar and place on serving plate.

Very pretty. This has a rich mocha filling, crusty crust, and just the right amount of sweetness from the light sprinkling of powdered sugar.

❦MOM'S HOLIDAY CINNAMON BISCUITS❦

4   1/2 cups prepared biscuit mix
1   1/3 cup milk

   1/2 cup melted butter

    1 cup sugar
    4 tsp. cinnamon

Preheat oven to 350 degrees.

Melt butter in shallow bowl. Set aside.

Mix sugar and cinnamon together in shallow bowl. Set aside.

Butter two 9-inch pie plates.

Prepare biscuits by stirring together biscuit mix and milk until soft dough forms. Turn onto surface dusted with baking mix. Knead 10 times.

Roll dough 1/2 inch thick. Cut with 2 1/2 inch cutter. Makes 24-26 biscuits (may vary).

Dip biscuit in warm butter, making sure all sides are coated. Then roll biscuit in cinnamon/sugar mixture. Place biscuit toward outside edge of pie plate. Repeat with next biscuit, slightly overlapping first biscuit, continuing in a circular manner until the biscuits meet. Place three biscuits in the center, each overlapping the next. Repeat with second pie plate.

Bake for approximately 30 minutes or until center biscuit is baked through.

Note: To prevent edges from burning, put strips of foil loosely around outside edge of plate, partially covering outside edge of biscuits.

Mom (Grace Bonn) made these as far back as I can remember for Easter Sunday breakfast. My family always requests them on Christmas and Easter. My sister makes them for her family, too. They are incredible!

❧MRS. BLAIR'S COFFEE CAKE❧

Cake:
>   1 cup brown sugar
>   1/2 cup sugar
> 2 1/2 cups flour
>   1 tsp. cinnamon
>   1/2 tsp. allspice
>   1/2 tsp. nutmeg
>   1/2 cup oil or melted butter
>   1 cup buttermilk
>   1 tsp. soda
>   3/4 tsp. salt
>   1 egg

Topping:
1 1/2 cups of the first seven ingredients, loosely packed
>   nuts, chopped (opt.)

Preheat oven to 350 degrees.

For the batter, stir together brown sugar, sugar, flour, cinnamon, allspice, and nutmeg. Stir in the oil or butter and **remove 1 1/2 cups, loosely packed, for topping. Set aside.**

To the remaining batter, add buttermilk, soda, salt, and egg. Stir until smooth. Pour batter into greased 9x13-inch pan.

Combine saved topping ingredients with chopped nuts. Sprinkle over the top. Bake for 25 minutes.

Linda Westeren gave me this recipe. She and her family have had it forever...who is Mrs. Blair? Great cake!

৶NECTARINE COFFEE CAKE৶

Dough:
  2 cups flour
  1 T. baking powder
1/2 tsp. salt
1/4 cup sugar
1/3 cup shortening or butter
  1 egg
    milk

Topping:
  2 nectarines, peeled, pitted, and sliced
  3 T. light-brown sugar

Preheat oven to 375 degrees.

Sift together the flour, baking powder, salt, and sugar. With a pastry blender or two knives, cut in shortening. Break the egg into measuring cup and beat lightly. Add milk to make 2/3 cup. Stir into dry ingredients, mixing well. Turn onto floured board and knead 30 seconds.

Press into a greased 9x9-inch pan. Arrange nectarine slices over the top and sprinkle with the brown sugar. Bake 25 minutes or until done.

⮞OLD-FASHIONED COFFEE CAKE⮜

Cake:
    1 cup butter, softened
1 1/4 cups sugar
    1 tsp. vanilla
    2 eggs
    1 cup sour cream
    2 cups flour
1 1/2 tsp. baking powder
    1/2 tsp. baking soda
    1 tsp. salt

Filling/Topping:
    1 cup chopped nuts (opt.)
    2 T. sugar
    1 tsp. cinnamon

Glaze:
    1/3 cup orange juice
    2 T. dark-brown sugar

Preheat oven to 350 degrees.

For cake, blend together butter and sugar; beat until light and fluffy. Add vanilla. Add eggs one at a time, beating well after each addition. Blend in sour cream. In a separate bowl, sift together flour, baking powder, baking soda, and salt. Gradually add to creamed mixture and beat until well blended. Spoon half of the batter into a greased 10-inch tube pan.

For topping, mix nuts, sugar, and cinnamon together. Sprinkle half of the mixture over batter. Top with remaining batter and sprinkle with remaining nut mixture. With a knife, cut through batter several times to marble slightly.

Bake 40 to 50 minutes. Cool on wire rack 10 minutes. Remove from pan and place on serving plate.

For glaze, combine orange juice and brown sugar in a saucepan; cook over low heat until sugar is dissolved. Brush over top and sides of warm cake. Serve warm.

Wonderfully moist and light. The orange glaze adds a delicious touch of citrus and sweet. Because of the glaze, this cake will stay moist longer.

⋦ORANGE COFFEE CAKE⋧

Cake:
1/2 cup light corn syrup
  1 tsp. grated orange peel
1/2 cup orange juice
1/4 cup butter, melted
  2 eggs, well beaten
  1 tsp. vanilla
  2 cups flour
1/2 tsp. salt
  1 T. baking powder

Topping:
  2 T. grated orange peel
1/2 cup sugar
  1 tsp. cinnamon
  1 T. butter, melted

Preheat oven to 375 degrees.

Combine corn syrup, orange peel, orange juice, and melted butter; mix thoroughly. Stir in eggs and vanilla. Sift flour with salt and baking powder into a mixing bowl; add to butter mixture. Pour into a greased and floured 8-inch square baking pan.

For topping, combine grated orange peel, sugar, cinnamon, and butter. Sprinkle over batter.

Bake for 30 minutes or until toothpick inserted into the center of the cake comes out clean.

❧ORANGE PINEAPPLE COFFEE CAKE❧

Cake:
1 1/2 cups flour
    1 cup whole wheat flour
    1/3 cup brown sugar, firmly packed
    3 tsp. baking powder
    1/2 tsp. baking soda
    1/4 tsp. salt
    2/3 cup crushed pineapple
    1/2 cup orange juice
    1/3 cup butter, melted
    1 tsp. grated orange peel
    1 egg, slightly beaten

Glaze:
    1/2 cup powdered sugar
    1 tsp. grated orange peel
    1 to 2 T. orange juice

Preheat oven to 400 degrees.

For cake, in large bowl, combine flour, whole wheat flour, brown sugar, baking powder, baking soda, and salt, thoroughly blending. In medium bowl, combine pineapple, orange juice, butter, orange peel, and egg; stir until blended. Add to dry ingredients all at once. Stir with wooden spoon until just moistened. Spread batter in greased 9-inch springform pan or 9-inch round cake pan.

Bake for 22 to 27 minutes or until toothpick inserted in center comes out clean. Cool slightly; remove from pan.

For glaze, in small bowl, combine powdered sugar, orange peel, and 1 to 2 tablespoons or enough orange juice to make drizzling consistency. Drizzle over warm cake. Serve warm.

❧OVERNIGHT CRUNCH COFFEE CAKE❧

Cake:
   2/3 cup butter, softened
   1 cup sugar
   1/2 cup firmly packed brown sugar
   2 eggs
2 1/4 cups flour
   1 tsp. baking powder
   1 tsp. baking soda
   1/4 tsp. salt
   1 tsp. cinnamon
   1 cup buttermilk

Topping #1:
   1/2 cup brown sugar, firmly packed
   1/2 cup chopped walnuts, (opt.)
   1/2 tsp. nutmeg
   1/2 tsp. cinnamon

Topping #2:
   1/2 cup brown sugar
   1/4 cup flour
   1 tsp. cinnamon
   1/2 tsp. instant coffee
   2 T. melted butter
   1/4 cup corn flakes, crushed

Topping #3:
   1/2 cup brown sugar
   1/2 cup walnuts or pecans, chopped (opt.)
   1/2 tsp. nutmeg
   1/4 cup butter, melted

For cake, on medium speed of an electric mixer, cream butter, gradually adding sugar and brown sugar. Beat well; add eggs, one at a time, beating after each addition. Stir together until thoroughly combined, the flour, baking powder, soda, salt, and cinnamon. Add flour mixture to creamed mixture alternately with buttermilk, beginning and ending with flour mixture. Pour batter into a greased and floured 9x13-inch baking pan.

Choose one topping and mix all ingredients together. Sprinkle topping evenly over batter. Cover and chill 8 hours. Bake at 350 degrees for 35 to 45 minutes or until lightly browned and tests done.

A keeper, this one is...very good, basic. Everyone will like it!

⟡OVERNIGHT CINNAMON COFFEE CAKE⟡

      1 package frozen dinner rolls
3 1/2 oz. instant butterscotch pudding
   1 cup brown sugar, firmly packed
   2 T. cinnamon
1/2 cup butter, melted
1/2 cup pecans

Preheat oven to 350 degrees.

In a greased bundt pan, layer in the following order: frozen rolls, powdered pudding, brown sugar, cinnamon, melted butter, and pecans. Cover the pan with foil. Over this place a clean towel and allow to sit overnight. Do not refrigerate.

Bake for 30 minutes or until done.

✑ORANGE BUTTERMILK COFFEE CAKE✑

Cake:
1 orange, pulp & rind
raisins, to taste
1/2 cup shortening or butter
1 cup sugar
2 eggs, beaten
1 tsp. vanilla
2 cups flour
1 tsp. baking soda
1/16 tsp. salt
1 cup buttermilk or sour milk (1 tsp. vinegar + 1 cup milk)
1/2 cup walnuts (opt.)

Glaze:
1/2 cup sugar
Juice from 1 orange

Preheat oven to 350 degrees.

Squeeze the juice from the orange; set aside. Grind the orange pulp and rind; set aside. Pour boiling water over raisins, then grind; set aside.

Cream shortening or butter; add sugar. Add beaten eggs; mix thoroughly; add vanilla. Stir together flour, baking soda, and salt. Add to creamed mixture, alternately with buttermilk. Beat until thoroughly mixed. Mixing after each addition, add orange pulp and rind. Add raisins. Add walnuts. Pour into greased 9x13-inch pan. Bake for 45-50 minutes, or until tests done.

Mix sugar and juice together and, using a spoon, pour slowly over hot cake as soon as it comes out of the oven.

This is an old, old recipe from my great-aunt Louise Brogan.

PEACH RASPBERRY UPSIDE-DOWN COFFEE CAKE

Cake:
   2 cups flour
   1 T. baking powder
1/4 tsp. salt
   2 T. sugar
1/3 cup butter
   1 egg
   1 cup milk

Topping:
1/4 cup melted butter
1/4 cup brown sugar, firmly packed
1/4 tsp. cinnamon
1/4 tsp. nutmeg
   2 cups fresh, frozen or canned peaches, thinly sliced

Filling:
1/3 cup sour cream
1/2 cup raspberry preserves

Preheat oven to 350 degrees.

For the cake, sift together the flour, baking powder, salt, and sugar in a large bowl. Cut in the butter using pastry blender. Beat the egg with the milk; add to the flour mixture. Stir just until mixed. Set aside.

For topping, combine the melted butter, brown sugar, cinnamon, and nutmeg; sprinkle on the bottom of a 9-inch square baking pan. Arrange the peach slices in rows. Spoon half of the batter over the peaches. Mix together the sour cream and the raspberry preserves and pour over batter. Spoon the remaining batter over preserves mixture and smooth.

Bake for 40 to 50 minutes or until done. Cool 15 minutes on a wire rack. Invert cake onto a plate. Carefully remove pan. Serve warm.

❧PEAR ALMOND COFFEE CAKE❧

Cake:
>   1/2 cup butter, softened
>   1 cup sugar
>   1/2 cup milk
>   2 eggs
> 1 1/2 tsp. vanilla
>   1/2 tsp. almond extract
>   2 cups flour
> 2 1/4 tsp. baking powder
>   1/4 tsp. salt

Topping:
>   2 medium pears, such as Anjou or Bartlett
>   1/3 cup apple jelly
>   1 T. sliced almonds

Preheat oven to 450 degrees.

In large bowl, beat the butter, adding sugar, milk, eggs, vanilla, and almond extract. In small bowl, mix flour, baking powder, and salt. Add to butter mixture. Beat on medium speed for 2 minutes or until smooth. Spread batter in a greased and floured 8-inch springform pan.

Peel, quarter, and core the pears. Cut each pear quarter into 1/2 inch-thick (or less) wedges. Arrange the pear wedges overlapping slightly in a circular pattern over the batter. Brush the pears with **half** the apple jelly. Sprinkle the almonds around the edge and in the center of the cake.

Bake for 15 minutes. Reduce the oven temperature to 350 degrees. Bake for 50 to 60 minutes longer, or until a toothpick inserted near the center comes out clean.

Set the pan on a wire rack to cool for 15 minutes. Remove the side of the pan and brush the top of the cake with the remaining apple jelly. Cool completely on the rack.

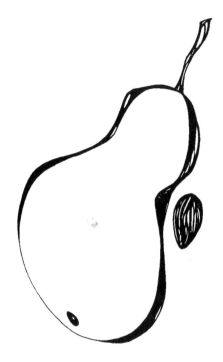

﹖PECAN CRUMBCAKE﹖

Cake:
    3 cups flour
1 1/2 cups sugar
  2/3 cup quick-cooking or old-fashioned oats, uncooked
    1 T. baking powder
    1 tsp. salt
  10 T. butter (1 stick, plus 2 T.)
    4 eggs
1 1/2 cup milk

Topping:
  1/4 cup packed brown sugar
  3/4 tsp. cinnamon
    1 cup flour
    6 T. butter
  1/2 cup pecans, chopped (opt.)

Preheat oven to 375 degrees.

For cake, in a large bowl, mix flour, sugar, oats, baking powder, and salt. With pastry blender or 2 knives used scissors fashion, cut in butter until mixture resembles course crumbs. In small bowl, beat eggs with milk until blended; stir into flour mixture just until flour is moistened. Spoon batter into a greased 9x13-inch pan, or two 8x8-inch pans.

For topping, in a medium-sized bowl, stir brown sugar, cinnamon, and flour. With pastry blender or 2 knives used scissors fashion, cut butter into flour mixture until mixture resembles large crumbs. Stir in pecans. Sprinkle pecan mixture over top of batter.

This is an old-fashioned, hearty, not-too-sweet cake - great reheated by the piece in the microwave with a dab of butter!

PECAN SOUR CREAM COFFEE CAKE

Cake:
1/2 cup butter, softened
1 cup sugar
3 eggs
2 cups flour
1 tsp. baking powder
1 tsp. baking soda
1/4 tsp. salt
1 cup sour cream
1/2 cup golden raisins

Topping:
3/4 cup brown sugar, firmly packed
1 T. flour
1 tsp. cinnamon
2 T. butter
1 cup chopped pecans (opt.)

Preheat oven to 325 degrees.

For cake, cream butter and sugar together; add eggs, one at a time, beating after each addition. Sift flour with baking powder, baking soda, and salt. Add to creamed mixture alternately with sour cream, blending after each addition. Stir in raisins. Spread in greased 9x13-inch baking pan.

For topping, combine brown sugar, flour, and cinnamon, mixing well. Cut in butter until crumbly. Mix in pecans. Sprinkle topping over cake.

Bake for about 30 minutes or until tests done.

Light and airy - sweet, but not too sweet. This cake is great even without raisins or pecans. Try Craisins (dried, sweetened cranberries) in place of the golden raisins.

❧PINEAPPLE UPSIDE-DOWN COFFEE CAKE❧

Cake:
1 1/3 cups sifted flour
  2/3 cup sugar
    2 tsp. baking powder
  2/3 cup buttermilk
  1/4 cup butter, melted
    2 eggs
1 1/2 tsp. vanilla
  1/4 tsp. coconut extract (opt.)

Topping:
    16 oz. pineapple slices, drained
12 to 20 pecan halves, unbroken
    1 T. butter, melted
    1 cup dark-brown sugar, loosely packed

Preheat oven to 350 degrees.

Combine flour, sugar, and baking powder in a large bowl; mix well. In another large bowl, stir together the buttermilk, butter, eggs, vanilla, and coconut extract. Stir the liquid ingredients into the dry ingredients and beat for 2 minutes, blending well.

Lightly grease with butter the bottom and sides of a 12-inch skillet, or 10-inch square, or 9x13-inch baking pan . Arrange the pineapple slices in the bottom of the pan. Place a pecan half, rounded side down in the center of each ring, in between the rings, and at the edges of the rings.

Drizzle the butter over the pineapple and nuts. Sprinkle with brown sugar. Pour the batter into the pan, making sure all the nuts, brown sugar, and pineapple are covered.

Bake for 40 to 50 minutes, or until done. Cool on wire rack for 15 to 20 minutes. Loosen edge of cake by sliding a flat rubber spatula around the edges of the cake. Invert the cake onto the plate by placing a larger serving plate on top of the pan, and quickly turning it over. Remove any pineapple rings, nuts, or brown sugar stuck to the cake pan and place it back on the cake. Serve warm or cold.

Wonderful breakfast version of an all-time favorite – not as sweet as a dessert.

❧PINEAPPLE COFFEE CAKE❧

Cake:
1/2 cup butter, softened
   1 cup brown sugar, firmly packed
   2 eggs
   1 tsp. vanilla
   2 cups flour
   1 tsp. baking soda
   1 tsp. baking powder
1/4 tsp. salt
   1 cup sour cream

Filling:
   1 cup crushed pineapple, drained

Topping:
1/4 cup sugar
1/3 cup brown sugar, firmly packed
1/2 cup chopped walnuts (opt.)
1/4 tsp. cinnamon
1/4 tsp. nutmeg

Preheat oven to 350 degrees.

For the cake, cream together the butter and brown sugar. Add the eggs and beat well. Add the vanilla; mix well. Mix together the flour, baking soda, baking powder, and salt. Add alternately to the butter mixture with the sour cream. Pour half the batter into a well-greased 9x13-inch pan. Spread the pineapple over this, then add the remaining batter.

For the topping, combine the sugar, brown sugar, walnuts, cinnamon, and nutmeg. Sprinkle over the batter. Bake for 25 to 30 minutes, or until done.

This is delicious, with just a hint of pineapple.

PLUM PEACH COFFEE CAKE

Cake:
30 to 31 oz. can whole purple plums, drained
1 cup butter, softened
1 cup sugar
4 eggs
2 tsp. grated lemon peel
1 3/4 cups flour
2 tsp. baking powder
1/8 tsp. salt

Topping:
1/2 cup butter, melted
1 cup flour
1/4 cup sugar
1 T. grated lemon peel

16 oz. can cling peaches, drained

Preheat oven to 325 degrees.

Cut each plum in half; discard pit. Set aside.

For cake, in large bowl of electric mixer, cream butter and sugar until light and fluffy. Add eggs, one at a time; beat until blended; add grated lemon peel. Combine flour, baking powder, and salt; add to butter mixture. Beat until smooth. Spread batter in greased and floured 9x13-inch pan. Top with half of the plums.

For topping, melt butter; stir in flour, sugar, and grated lemon peel to form a soft dough. Pinch topping into small pieces and sprinkle on top of cake. Bake 20 minutes. Quickly top cake with peaches and remaining plums. Bake 30 to 35 minutes longer until toothpick inserted in center comes out clean. Serve warm or cool.

❧POPPY SEED BREAD❧

3 1/3 cups flour
    1 cup + 1 T. sugar
    4 tsp. baking powder
  1/2 tsp. salt
    2 oz. poppy seeds
    1 cup + 2 T. vegetable oil
1 1/2 cups milk
1 1/2 tsp. vanilla
    3 eggs

Preheat oven to 350 degrees.

Mix flour, sugar, baking powder, salt, and poppy seeds together in a bowl. Blend well and then add oil, milk, vanilla, and eggs. Mix thoroughly together at medium speed on mixer until smooth, approximately 4 minutes. Scrape sides of bowl often. Pour into 2 greased loaf pans, 8 1/2x4 1/2. Bake for approximately 1 hour.

NOTE: May pour batter into greased muffin tins for Poppy Seed Muffins. 18 large muffins.

This bread is so good, light, and sweet! Great for breakfast, toasted with butter.

PULL-APART COFFEE CAKE

Cake:
    1 loaf frozen white bread dough
   1/4 cup butter, melted
   1/2 cup sugar
    2 tsp. cinnamon

Glaze:
    1 cup confectioner's sugar
1 1/2 T. milk
    1 drop almond extract
    1 drop coconut extract

For cake, thaw one loaf of frozen white bread dough according to package instructions. Melt butter in a bowl. In a separate bowl, mix sugar and cinnamon. Make about 17 individual balls of dough the size of golf balls. Roll in the melted butter, then roll in the cinnamon and sugar mixture. Arrange in a greased 9-inch cake pan. Put in a warm place and allow to rise and double or triple in size. Bake in preheated 350 degree oven for 10 to 15 minutes.

For glaze, combine the confectioner's sugar, milk, almond extract, and coconut extract. Drizzle over the top of warm cake.

You may leave off the glaze or cut down on the amount, if you don't care for the extra sweetness.

‿PRUNE APRICOT COFFEE CAKE‿

Cake:
3/4 cup dried prunes
3/4 cup dried apricots
3/4 cup butter, softened
3/4 cup sugar
  2 eggs
  1 tsp. vanilla
  2 cups sifted flour
  2 tsp. baking powder
1/2 tsp. salt
3/4 cup milk

Topping:
2/3 cup light-brown sugar, firmly packed
  1 T. flour
  1 T. cinnamon
  6 T. butter, melted and separated
1/3 cup chopped walnuts

Preheat oven to 350 degrees.

Let prunes and apricots stand in hot water, covered, 5 minutes. Drain; chop finely; set aside.

For cake, in a large bowl, beat at medium speed butter and sugar until light and fluffy. Beat in eggs, one at a time, beating well after each addition; add vanilla. Into medium bowl, sift flour with baking powder and salt. At low speed, add flour mixture alternately with milk. Beat just to combine. Gently fold in fruit. Spread one third of the batter into a greased and floured 9-inch tube pan.

For topping, combine brown sugar with flour and cinnamon, mixing well. Sprinkle one third over the batter. Then sprinkle one third of the melted butter over this (2 tablespoons). Repeat layering batter, topping, and butter twice. Over the top sprinkle chopped nuts. Bake 55 minutes, or until toothpick comes out clean. Let cool.

PRUNE NUT COFFEE RING

Filling:
    1/2 cup pitted prunes, chopped
      3 T. water
      1 T. lemon juice
    1/4 cup sugar
    3/4 tsp. lemon rind, grated
    1/2 tsp. vanilla
    1/4 tsp. cloves

Dough:
    1 loaf frozen sweet dough, thawed
    1/2 cup walnuts, chopped (opt.)

Glaze:
1 1/2 cups powdered sugar
    3/4 tsp. vanilla
      3 T. milk

Preheat oven to 350 degrees.

For filling, combine prunes, water, and lemon juice in a small saucepan. Bring to a boil over medium heat; reduce heat to low, cover, and simmer for 5 minutes or until prunes are very soft. Stir in sugar and remove from heat. Stir in lemon rind, vanilla, and cloves. Cool completely. To speed cooling, place in refrigerator.

On a lightly floured surface, roll dough to a 10x18-inch rectangle. Spread prune filling evenly over the surface, within 1/2 inch of the edges. Sprinkle walnuts over the filling. From the long side, roll the dough like a jelly roll. Seal the edge well. Place on greased baking sheet, seam side down, to form a ring, ends meeting. To seal, moisten ends slightly and pinch together. With scissors or very sharp knife, make cuts from outer edge to within 3/4 inch of center at 1-inch intervals. Twist each section slightly so filling shows. Cover and let rise in a warm place until doubled, about an hour. Bake for 30 minutes or until golden. Place on wire rack.

For glaze, mix powdered sugar, vanilla, and enough of the 3 tablespoons of milk for drizzling consistency. Stir until smooth. Drizzle over cake while warm. Serve warm or at room temperature with butter. Best eaten within a few hours.

❧PUMPKIN BREAD❧

1 1/2 cup pumpkin
1 3/4 cup sugar
  1/2 cup oil
2 3/4 cups sifted flour
1 1/2 tsp. soda
  3/4 tsp. salt
    1 tsp. cinnamon
  1/4 tsp. allspice
  1/4 tsp. cloves
  1/2 tsp. pumpkin pie spice
    1 cup chopped nuts (opt.)

Preheat oven to 350 degrees.

Mix all ingredients together; stir until thoroughly combined. Pour into greased loaf pan. Bake 1 hour.

Simple to make, but so delicious! Try toasting a cold slice and putting a little butter on it. Mmmmm...

QUICK COFFEE CAKE

Cake:
   2 cups flour
1/4 cup sugar
   1 T. baking powder
1/4 tsp. salt
1/4 cup shortening or butter
3/4 cup milk
   1 egg yolk, beaten

Topping:
   3 T. butter, softened
1/4 cup flour
1/4 cup sugar
   1 tsp. cinnamon

Preheat oven to 375 degrees.

For cake, mix flour, sugar, baking powder, and salt; cut in shortening with pastry blender or two knives. Stir egg yolk into milk and add to dry ingredients. Spread in greased 9x13-inch pan.

For topping, mix butter, flour, sugar, and cinnamon. Sprinkle over top. Bake 25 to 30 minutes.

NOTE: May substitute 2 cups prepared biscuit mix plus 1/4 cup of sugar for first 5 ingredients.

This is a nice, light, tasty cake.

❧QUICK SWEDISH TEA RING❧

Dough:
   2 cups flour
   1 T. baking powder
1/2 tsp. salt
1/4 cup shortening
3/4 cup milk (approx.)
      -OR-
   2 cups prepared biscuit mix
3/4 cup milk (approx.)

Filling:
1/3 cup butter, softened
1/4 cup firmly packed brown sugar
  1 tsp. cinnamon
1/2 cup chopped almonds (opt.)

Preheat oven to 400 degrees.

For dough, combine flour, baking powder, and salt; cut in shortening until well mixed and add milk, stirring until a soft, (but not sticky) dough is formed. Turn out on lightly floured board and knead just enough to shape into smooth ball, 10 to 15 times. Roll dough to a rectangle, 1/3 inch thick.

For filling, spread butter over the dough. Mix together brown sugar, cinnamon, and almonds. Sprinkle over dough. Roll lengthwise, jelly-roll style, place on greased baking sheet and seal ends to form a ring. With scissors or very sharp knife, cut 3/4-inch slices almost to center, turning each slice over on flat side to show filling. Bake for about 25 minutes or until done.

↬RAISIN SPICE COFFEE CAKE↫

Cake:
   2 cups sifted flour
   1 T. baking powder
1/2 tsp. salt
1/2 cup sugar
   1 tsp. cinnamon
1/4 tsp. mace
1/3 cup butter
1/2 cup raisins, chopped
   1 egg
1/2 cup milk

Topping:
   1 T. butter, melted and
   2 T. butter, melted
   2 T. sugar
1/2 tsp. cinnamon
1/2 cup crushed corn flakes

Preheat oven to 350 degrees.

For cake, sift flour, baking powder, salt, sugar, cinnamon, and
mace into large bowl. Cut in butter with pastry blender or use 2
knives, scissors fashion, until mixture looks like course corn meal.
Add raisins. Into small bowl, beat egg; add milk; mix well. Stir
into flour mixture until just mixed. Pour into greased 8x8-inch
square or 9-inch pie plate.

For topping, brush batter with 1 tablespoon melted butter, using
a pastry brush or crumpled waxed paper. Mix together 2 T.
butter, sugar, cinnamon, and corn flakes. Sprinkle topping over
cake. Bake 25 to 30 minutes, or until cake tests done.

NOTE: To make Crumb Cake, omit raisins, 1 tsp. cinnamon and
1/4 tsp. mace.

ᔕRAISIN-FILLED COFFEE CAKEᔓ

Filling:
   1 T. cornstarch
1/2 cup water
1/2 cup chopped walnuts, (opt.)
1/2 cup sugar
   1 cup raisins
    Grated peel and juice of 1 small lemon

Cake:
1/2 cup butter
1/4 cup sugar
1/2 cup brown sugar, firmly packed
1/2 tsp. vanilla
   2 eggs
   2 cups sifted flour
   2 tsp. baking powder
1/4 tsp. salt
1/2 cup milk

Topping:
   2 T. melted butter
1/4 tsp. cinnamon
   2 T. sugar

Preheat oven to 350 degrees.

For filling, in saucepan, dissolve cornstarch in cold water. Add walnuts, sugar, raisins, lemon peel, and lemon juice. Bring to a boil over medium heat, stirring constantly. Cool in refrigerator.

Cream together butter, sugar, and brown sugar; add vanilla. Add eggs and beat mixture until light and fluffy. Sift flour with baking powder and salt. Add flour mixture and milk alternately, stirring after each addition.

Spread half the batter in a greased 8-inch square baking pan. Spread raisin filling over the batter, and then spread remaining batter carefully over filling. Brush with melted butter.

For topping, combine butter, cinnamon, and sugar. Sprinkle over batter. Bake for about 30 minutes. Cool before serving.

I first made this cake when I was 15 years old. A must for raisin lovers.

✓ ~RASPBERRY CREAM CHEESE COFFEE CAKE~

Cake:
2 1/2 cups flour
   3/4 cup sugar
   3/4 cup butter
   1/2 tsp. baking powder
   1/2 tsp. baking soda
   1/4 tsp. salt
   3/4 cup sour cream
      1 egg
      1 tsp almond extract

Filling:
      8 oz. cream cheese, softened
   1/4 cup sugar
      1 egg
1/2-3/4 cup raspberry jam

Topping:
      1 cup reserved crumbs
   1/2 cup sliced almonds

Preheat oven to 350 degrees.

For cake, combine flour and sugar. Cut in butter with pastry blender or two knives until mixture resembles course crumbs. **Set aside 1 cup of crumbs for topping**. Add baking powder, baking soda, salt, sour cream, egg, and almond extract to remaining crumbs. Mix well. Spread batter over bottom and 2 inches up the sides of a greased and floured 9-inch springform pan.

For filling, blend cream cheese, sugar, and egg. Beat until smooth. Pour over the batter. Carefully spread the raspberry jam over cheese filling.

For topping, mix reserved crumbs and sliced almonds. Sprinkle over top of cake. Bake 40-50 minutes or until cheese filling is set and crust is a golden brown. Cool 10-15 minutes before removing sides of pan.

My sister, Louise Bonn Johnson, gave me this recipe. It looks so elegant and it tastes wonderful! Thanks, sis.

❧RASPBERRY PASTRY❧

Dough:
    2 cups biscuit mix
    3 oz. cream cheese
  1/3 cup milk
  1/3 cup raspberry preserves

Icing:
  3/4 cup powdered sugar
  1/2 tsp. vanilla
1 to 3 tsp. milk
    1 T. sliced almonds, toasted (opt.)

Preheat oven to 425 degrees.

For dough, measure biscuit mix into a medium mixing bowl, cut in cream cheese with pastry blender or two knives until crumbly. Add milk and stir until mixed. On a lightly floured surface, knead gently 8 to 10 times.

Roll dough to a 8x12-inch rectangle on waxed paper. Turn onto a greased baking sheet; remove paper. Spread preserves down center of the dough. Make 2 1/2-inch long cuts, at 1-inch intervals, from edges of long sides toward the center. Starting at one end, alternately fold opposite strips of dough, at an angel, across the filling. Slightly press ends together in the center to seal. Bake for 15 to 17 minutes or until golden brown.

For icing, in a small mixing bowl, stir together powdered sugar, vanilla, and enough milk (1 to 3 teaspoons) to make it drizzling consistency. Drizzle over warm pastry. Sprinkle with almonds.

ᵕRHUBARB CAKEᵕ

Cake:
   1/2 cup butter, softened
1 1/2 cup brown sugar
     1 egg
     1 cup sour milk or buttermilk
     1 tsp. vanilla
     2 cups flour
     1 tsp. baking soda
   1/4 tsp. salt
1 1/2 to 2 cups rhubarb, raw, chopped in 1/2 inch pieces

Topping:
   1/4 cup sugar
     1 tsp. cinnamon

Preheat oven to 350 degrees.

For cake, cream together butter and brown sugar; add egg. Add sour milk and vanilla. Combine flour, baking soda, and salt; add to butter mixture. Blend together and stir in rhubarb. Pour into a greased 9x13-inch baking pan.

For topping, combine sugar and cinnamon. Sprinkle over batter. Bake for 30 minutes.

NOTE: Make sour milk by combining 1 cup milk and 1 T. vinegar.

This recipe came from Rosanna Duberow, a long-time and very special friend of the family.

RHUBARB STRAWBERRY COFFEE CAKE

Filling:
   3 cups fresh rhubarb, cut in 1-inch pieces
   16 oz. package frozen sliced sweetened strawberries, thawed
   1 cup sugar
1/3 cup cornstarch

Cake:
   3 cups flour
   1 cup sugar
   1 tsp. baking soda
   1 tsp. baking powder
   1 tsp. salt
1/8 tsp. cinnamon
   1 cup butter
   1 cup buttermilk
   2 eggs, slightly beaten
   1 tsp. almond extract

Topping:
3/4 cup sugar
1/2 cup flour
1/4 cup butter
1/4 cup flaked coconut

Preheat oven to 350 degrees.

For filling, combine the rhubarb and strawberries in a saucepan and cook about 5 minutes. Combine the sugar and cornstarch and stir into fruit. Cook until bubbly and thick. Set aside to cool. May refrigerate to speed cooling.

For cake, in a large mixing bowl, combine flour, sugar, soda, baking powder, salt, and cinnamon. Cut in butter using a pastry blender or two knives until the mixture resembles fine crumbs. In a separate bowl, beat together the buttermilk, eggs, and almond extract. Add this to the flour mixture, stirring just to moisten. Spread half of the batter in a greased 9x13-inch pan. Spread the cooled rhubarb filling over this and spoon the remaining batter in small mounds on top of the filling.

For the topping, combine sugar and flour. Using a pastry blender or two knives, cut in butter until the mixture resembles fine crumbs. Add the flaked coconut. Sprinkle the topping over the batter. Bake for 40 to 45 minutes, or until done.

RHUBARB COFFEE CAKE

Cake:
   2/3 cup oil
1 1/2 cups brown sugar, firmly packed
      1 egg
      1 tsp. vanilla
2 1/2 cups sifted flour
      1 tsp. baking soda
      1 tsp. salt
      1 cup milk
1 1/2 cups chopped rhubarb
      1/2 cup sliced almonds

Topping:
      1/2 cup sugar
      1 T. butter, melted
      1/4 cup sliced almonds

Preheat oven to 350 degrees.

For cake, stir together oil, brown sugar, egg, and vanilla until thoroughly mixed. Combine flour, baking soda, and salt; add to the oil mixture alternately with milk. Stir in rhubarb and almonds. Pour into a greased and floured 9x13-inch pan.

For topping, combine sugar, butter, and almonds. Sprinkle over batter. Bake for 40 to 45 minutes, or until done.

❧SIMPLE COFFEE CAKE❧

    1/3 cup soft shortening or butter, softened
    1/3 cup sugar
      1 egg
    2/3 cup milk
      2 cups sifted flour
2 1/2 tsp. baking powder
    3/4 tsp. salt

Preheat oven to 375 degrees.

Cream shortening; add sugar and beat until light and fluffy. Add egg and beat well; add milk. Sift flour, baking powder, and salt together. Add to creamed mixture, and stir until just moistened. Pour into greased 8-inch square pan. Bake 20 to 25 minutes, or until done. Serve hot.

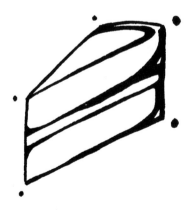

❧SNICKERDOODLE COFFEE CAKE❧

Cake:
        1 cup shortening
1 1/3 cups sugar
        2 eggs
2 2/3 cups flour
        4 tsp. baking powder
    1/2 tsp. salt
1 1/3 cups milk

Topping:
    1/4 cup sugar
        1 tsp. cinnamon

Preheat oven to 350 degrees.

In a large mixing bowl, cream together shortening and sugar until light and fluffy; beat in the eggs, one at a time. Sift together in another bowl, the flour, baking powder, and salt; add this alternately with milk into the egg mixture, beating until the batter is smooth. Pour batter into greased and floured 9x13-inch pan.

Bake for 45 minutes or until toothpick inserted in the center comes out clean.

Combine sugar and cinnamon and sprinkle over the top of the hot baked cake.

❧SOMEONE'S AUNT'S COFFEE CAKE❧

Cake:
  1/2 cup butter
  3/4 cup sugar
    1 egg
2 1/4 cups flour
    4 tsp. baking powder
  1/4 tsp. salt
    1 cup milk
  1/2 cup chopped dates
  1/2 cup chopped nuts
    1 tsp. grated orange rind

Topping:
  1/2 cup sugar
    2 tsp. cinnamon

Preheat oven to 350 degrees.

For cake, cream the butter and sugar together until light and fluffy. Beat in the egg. Sift the flour with the baking powder and salt. Add alternately with the milk to the batter. Fold in the dates, nuts, and orange rind. Spoon into a greased 9x9-inch pan.

For topping, mix sugar and cinnamon together, and sprinkle over cake. Bake 45 minutes, or until done. Serve warm.

&SOUR CREAM and BREAD CRUMBS CAKE&

Cake:
   3/4 cup butter, softened
1 1/2 cups sugar
3 to 4 eggs
1 1/2 cups sour cream
1 1/2 tsp. vanilla
      3 cups flour
1 1/2 tsp. baking powder
1 1/2 tsp. baking soda

Filling/Topping:
   3/4 cup dried bread crumbs
   1/2 cup flour
   1/3 cup sugar
1 1/2 tsp. cinnamon
   1/2 tsp. nutmeg
   1/2 cup butter, softened
     1 cup ground walnuts (opt.)

Preheat oven to 350 degrees.

For cake, in a large mixing bowl, beat butter and sugar until light and fluffy. Add eggs, one at a time; add sour cream and vanilla. Combine flour, baking powder, and baking soda; add to butter mixture. Beat at medium speed for 3 minutes. Spread one-third of the batter into a greased 10-inch tube pan.

For filling/topping, in a small mixing bowl, beat together at low speed the bread crumbs, flour, sugar, cinnamon, nutmeg, and butter until well blended. Stir in walnuts.

Sprinkle one-third of the crumb filling over the batter. Repeat with batter and filling two times. Bake for 50 to 60 minutes, until the cake tests done. Do not overbake.

❧SOUR CREAM CINNAMON COFFEE CAKE❧

Cake:
  4 eggs
1/2 cup sugar
3/4 cup oil
  1 package yellow cake mix
  1 cup sour cream
3/4 cup chopped nuts

Filling:
1/4 cup dark brown sugar
  1 T. cinnamon

Preheat oven to 350 degrees.

For cake, beat the eggs until thick and fluffy. Add the sugar and oil; beat again. Add the cake mix, sour cream, and nuts. Pour half of the batter into a well-greased and floured bundt pan.

For filling, mix together the brown sugar and cinnamon. Sprinkle over the batter. Swirl the filling slightly with a knife. Pour the remaining batter on top. Bake for 45 to 60 minutes, or until tests done. Cool for 10 minutes and invert on cake plate.

❧SOUR CREAM COFFEE CAKE❧

Cake:
1/2 cup butter
   1 cup sugar
   2 eggs
   1 tsp. vanilla
   2 cups sifted flour
   1 tsp. baking soda
   1 tsp. baking powder
   1 cup sour cream

Filling/Topping:
   4 T. sugar
   2 tsp. cinnamon
1/2 cup chopped nuts (opt.)
   3 T. butter, melted

Preheat oven to 350 degrees.

For the cake, cream together the butter and sugar; add the eggs one at a time, beating well. Add the vanilla. Combine flour, baking soda, and baking powder and add to butter mixture alternately with the sour cream. Beat until thoroughly blended. Pour half of the batter in a greased 10-inch tube pan.

For filling/topping, combine sugar, cinnamon, and chopped nuts. Sprinkle half over the batter. Pour the remaining batter over the top of this mixture. Pour the melted butter over the batter. Sprinkle the remaining topping over the butter. Bake for 50 to 55 minutes or until done. Let cool for 10 minutes. Invert to a cake plate.

❧STREUSEL COFFEE CAKE❧

Cake:
1 1/2 cups flour
   3/4 cup sugar
     2 tsp. baking powder
  1/2 tsp. salt
    1 egg, beaten
  1/2 cup milk
  1/4 cup oil
  1/2 cup raisins

Topping:
  1/2 cup nuts, chopped (opt.)
  1/4 cup brown sugar, firmly packed
    1 T. flour
    1 T. butter, softened
    1 tsp. cinnamon

Heat oven to 375 degrees.

For the cake, combine the flour, sugar, baking powder, and salt. Mix together egg, milk, and oil. Add to the flour mixture; mix until thoroughly combined. Stir in raisins. Pour into a greased 9x9-inch baking pan.

For topping, combine nuts, brown sugar, flour, butter, and cinnamon. Sprinkle over batter. Bake for 20 to 25 minutes or until tests done.

This cake is light, not-too-sweet, nice.

❧SOURDOUGH COFFEE CAKE❧

Cake:
1 1/4 cups flour
   1/2 cup sugar
1 1/2 tsp. baking powder
   1/8 tsp. salt
   1/4 cup butter
   2/3 cup sourdough starter *
     1 egg, beaten
     1 tsp. vanilla

Topping:
    21 oz. can cherry pie filling
   1/2 cup flour
   1/4 cup brown sugar, firmly packed
   1/2 tsp. cinnamon
   1/4 cup butter

Preheat oven to 350 degrees.

For cake, in a large mixing bowl combine flour, sugar, baking powder, and salt. Cut in butter with a pastry cutter or two knives until mixture resembles course crumbs. Stir together sourdough starter, egg, and vanilla. Add to dry ingredients; mix well. Spread in a greased 8x8-inch baking pan.

Spoon pie filling over batter. For topping, combine flour, brown sugar, and cinnamon. Cut in the butter with a pastry cutter or two knives until mixture resembles course crumbs; sprinkle over pie filling. Bake for 45 minutes, or until done. Cool on wire rack for at least 45 minutes.

* Sourdough Starter: Soften 1 package active dry yeast in 1/2 cup warm water (110 degrees). Stir in 2 cups warm water, 2 cups flour, and 1 tablespoon sugar. Beat until smooth. Cover with cheesecloth; let stand at room temperature 5 to 10 days,

stirring 2 or 3 times a day. Cover and refrigerate until ready to use.

To replenish starter after using part of it, add 3/4 cup water, 3/4 cup flour, and 1 teaspoon sugar to the starter. Let stand at room temperature until bubbly, at least 1 day. Cover and refrigerate for later use. If not used within 10 days, add 1 teaspoon sugar. Repeat adding sugar every 10 days.

Before using, measure the starter, then let it stand until it's at room temperature.

๛STREUSEL SOUR CREAM COFFEE CAKE๛

Cake:
  1/2 cup butter, softened
  3/4 cup sugar
    2 eggs
1 1/2 tsp. vanilla
    2 cups flour
1 1/2 tsp. baking powder
  3/4 tsp. baking soda
  1/4 tsp. salt
    1 cup sour cream

Streusel Filling/Topping:
  2/3 cup flour
  2/3 cup light-brown sugar, packed
  3/4 tsp. cinnamon
  1/8 tsp. nutmeg
  1/4 cup cold butter, cut into small pieces
  1/2 cup toasted walnuts, chopped (opt.)

Preheat oven to 350 degrees.

For the cake, in a large bowl, beat the butter and sugar with an electric mixer until light and fluffy. Beat in the eggs, one at a time, mixing thoroughly after each addition; add the vanilla. In a medium sized bowl, mix the flour, baking powder, baking soda, and salt. Add to butter mixture alternately with the sour cream; mix until well blended. Spread half of the mixture into a greased 9-inch springform pan.

For the streusel, mix flour, brown sugar, cinnamon, and nutmeg. Cut in the butter with a pastry blender or two knives until the mixture resembles course crumbs. Sprinkle 1/2 cup streusel over the batter in the pan. Spread the remaining batter over the top of the streusel. Add the walnuts to the remaining streusel mixture and sprinkle it over the top of the cake. Lightly pat the topping into the batter.

Bake 55 to 60 minutes, until a toothpick comes out clean. Cool for 10 minutes, then remove the sides of the pan. Let cool completely before serving.

*Deliciously **sweet**.*

❧STRUDEL❧

Cake:
- 1 cup butter, softened
- 2 cups sifted flour
- 2 T. water
- 2 T. white vinegar
- 3 egg yolks

Filling:
- 6 apples, peeled, cored, and diced
- 1 cup raisins
- 1 cup finely chopped nuts (opt.)
- 1/2 cup sugar
- 2 T. cinnamon

Icing:
- 3/4 cup confectioner's sugar
- 1 T. cream
- 1/2 tsp. almond extract

Preheat oven to 350 degrees.

For cake, thoroughly combine the butter, flour, water, vinegar, and egg yolks making a dough; refrigerate.

For the filling, combine apples, raisins, nuts, sugar, and cinnamon.

Separate the dough into two balls and on a lightly floured surface, roll each ball as thin as possible into a rectangle; spread with half the filling. Roll up jelly roll-style.

Bake on a lightly greased cookie sheet for 20 minutes or until brown.

For icing, combine confectioner's sugar, cream, and almond extract and drizzle over the top of warm strudel.

❧STREUSEL LAYERED COFFEE CAKE❧

Cake:
- 1 egg
- 3/4 cup sugar
- 1/3 cup butter, melted
- 1/2 cup milk
- 1 tsp. vanilla
- 1 1/2 cups sifted flour
- 2 1/2 tsp. baking powder
- 1/4 tsp. salt

Filling/Topping:
- 1/2 cup light-brown sugar, firmly packed
- 2 T. butter, softened
- 2 T. flour
- 1 tsp. cinnamon
- 1/2 cup coarsely chopped walnuts (opt.)

Preheat oven to 375 degrees.

For cake, in medium bowl, beat egg until frothy; then beat in sugar and butter until well combined. Add milk and vanilla. Sift flour with baking powder and salt; and with a wooden spoon, beat into egg mixture until well combined. Pour half the batter into a greased 8x8-inch pan or 9-inch round pan.

For streusel, in small bowl, combine brown sugar, butter, flour, cinnamon, and walnuts. Mix with fork, until crumbly. Sprinkle half the mixture evenly over batter. Repeat with batter and streusel.

Bake 25 to 30 minutes, or until toothpick inserted into center of cake comes out clean. Serve warm.

ꙮWALNUT COFFEE CAKEꙮ

Cake:
    3/4 cup butter, softened
      1 cup sugar
    1/2 cup brown sugar, firmly packed
      3 eggs
      1 tsp. vanilla
      2 cups flour
      1 cup whole wheat flour
      1 T. baking powder
    3/4 tsp. baking soda
    3/4 tsp. salt
1 1/2 cups sour cream

Filling/Topping:
    1/2 cup sugar
1 1/2 tsp. cinnamon
    1/2 cup finely chopped walnuts (opt.)
      2 T. butter, cut into small pieces
        powdered sugar

Preheat oven to 350 degrees.

For cake, beat butter at medium speed with an electric mixer until soft and creamy; gradually add sugar and brown sugar, beating mixture well. Add eggs, one at a time, beating after each addition. Stir in vanilla. Combine flour, whole wheat flour, baking powder, baking soda, and salt; add to butter mixture alternately with sour cream, beginning and ending with flour mixture. Mix after each addition. Spoon half the batter into a greased and floured bundt pan.

For filling/topping, combine sugar, cinnamon, and walnuts. Sprinkle half of nut mixture over the batter. Add remaining batter, spreading evenly, and top with remaining nut mixture. Place the small butter pieces around the top of the cake. Bake for 40 to 45 minutes or until a wooden pick inserted in center of cake comes out clean. Cool in pan on a wire rack 10 minutes; invert cake onto the wire rack. Using a sifter, sprinkle with powdered sugar.

*I prefer pecans over walnuts...but remember, nuts are **always** optional - even in a recipe with nuts in the name!*

❧SUNDAY MORNING BREAKFAST CAKE❧

Cake:
   2 eggs
   1 cup sugar
   1 tsp. vanilla
   1 cup sifted flour
   1 tsp. baking powder
1/4 tsp. salt
1/2 cup hot milk
   1 T. butter

Topping:
1/4 cup butter, softened
   2 T. cream or evaporated milk
2/3 cup brown sugar, firmly packed
   1 cup coarsely chopped walnuts (opt.)
     pinch salt

Preheat oven to 350 degrees.

For cake, beat eggs with electric mixer until very thick and lemon-colored, about 5 minutes. Continue beating eggs and slowly add sugar; add vanilla. Sift together flour, baking powder, and salt. Add to egg mixture. Drop butter into hot milk; when butter is melted, quickly stir into batter. Pour into greased pan, about 8x12-inches. Bake for 25 minutes or until done.

For topping, mix together butter, cream, and brown sugar, until smooth. Stir in nuts and salt. When cake is done, spread butter mixture on top, in pan. Broil until golden brown. Watch carefully so it doesn't burn - it won't take long. Serve hot or warm.

If you like caramel, you will enjoy this light, delicate cake.

ᏊZUCCHINI BREADᏊ

        3 eggs
2 1/4 cups sugar
        1 T. vanilla
        1 cup oil
        2 cups grated, pared zucchini
        3 cups flour
    1/4 tsp. baking powder
        1 tsp. salt
        1 tsp. baking soda
        1 T. cinnamon
        1 cup chopped nuts (opt.)

Preheat oven at 350 degrees.

Beat eggs until light and fluffy. Add sugar, vanilla, and oil. Blend well. Stir in grated zucchini.

Sift together flour, baking powder, salt, baking soda, and cinnamon. Blend with creamed mixture. Fold in chopped nuts. Pour into 2 greased and floured 9x5-inch loaf pans. Bake for 1 hour or until tests done.

One of my all-time favorite recipes. Incredible bread! Wonderful toasted with butter and served with breakfast.

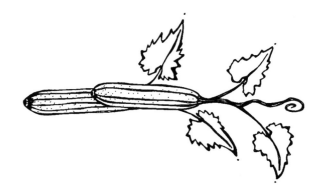

INDEX

To Order:

COFFEE CAKES 105 Wonderful Recipes

by Lauri Bonn

ᔕᔕᔕᔕᔕᔕᔕᔕᔕᔕᔕᔕᔕᔕᔕᔕᔕᔕᔕᔕᔕᔕ

Enclose check or money order for $15.00 plus $3.00 for shipping and handling for each book, made payable to Maren Publishing.

Total Number of books ordered_____

x $15.00 each_____

+ $3.00 s & h each book_____

Total Enclosed $ _____

ᔕᔕᔕᔕᔕᔕᔕᔕᔕᔕᔕᔕᔕᔕᔕᔕᔕᔕᔕᔕᔕᔕ

Name_____

Address_____

City_____

State_____Zip_____

Maren Publishing, PO Box 8205, Bend, OR 97708
(541) 383-2160 www.marenpublishing.com